The Grandparent Vocation

The
Grandparent Vocation

Wisdom, Legacies, and
Spiritual Growth

Richard P. Olson

ROWMAN & LITTLEFIELD
Lanham • Boulder • New York • London

Published by Rowman & Littlefield
An imprint of The Rowman & Littlefield Publishing Group, Inc.
4501 Forbes Boulevard, Suite 200, Lanham, Maryland 20706
www.rowman.com

86-90 Paul Street, London EC2A 4NE

British Library Cataloguing in Publication Information Available

Library of Congress Cataloging-in-Publication Data

Names: Olson, Richard P., author.
 Title: The Grandparent vocation : wisdom, legacies, and spiritual growth /
  Richard P. Olson.
 Description: Lanham : Rowman & Littlefield, [2022] | Includes
  bibliographical references and index.
 Identifiers: LCCN 2022028190 (print) | LCCN 2022028191 (ebook) | ISBN
  9781538164402 (cloth) | ISBN 9781538164419 (paperback) | ISBN
  9781538164426 (ebook)
 Subjects: LCSH: Grandparents--Religious life. | Grandparenting--Religious
  aspects--Christianity.
 Classification: LCC BV4528.5 .O425 2022 (print) | LCC BV4528.5 (ebook) |
  DDC 248.8/45--dc23/eng/20220815
 LC record available at https://lccn.loc.gov/2022028190
 LC ebook record available at https://lccn.loc.gov/2022028191

*This book is dedicated to Mary Ann's and my
grandchildren by birth and by marriage:
Daniel and Julia, Carolyn and Harrison, Audrey and Kevin,
Emma, Jeffrey, and Robyn;
and great-grandchildren, all little boys so far:
Crosby, Boden, Beckett, and Milo.
You are our beloved, our delight,
our concern, our worry,
our calling.*

Contents

Acknowledgments

I express my appreciation to the several persons at Rowman & Littlefield who have been so supportive through this endeavor. Acquisition editors Natalie Mandziuk and Richard Brown helped clarify my purpose and focus on this topic and say it as well as I could. Editorial assistants Sylvia Landis and Jaylene Perez were always so responsive, prompt, and informative. Crystal Branson guided me through the copy editing equally ably.

Deep thanks to the grandparents and grandchildren who visited with me in person or in writing. There were at least two dozen formal interviews framed by my set of questions and on which I took careful notes. Some of these volunteered in response to my requests in the retirement community where I live—Oakwood Village, Prairie Ridge, in Madison, Wisconsin. I recruited some others out of my awareness and admiration of their grandparenting experience. I also turned to professional colleagues to learn about the commonalities and distinctions in grandparenting across generational, racial, and ethnic differences.

There were many other informal conversations, when, perhaps, neither of us knew what I was doing. Funny, grandchildren just come up in our conversations! I enjoyed talking with each of you and wish I could have included all your stories!

A word about how I have treated names. By agreement, I used only a first name for each grandparent I interviewed and/or whose story I told. There was an additional initial when there were more than one with the same name. Stories out of books reported names in the way given there. I did not include the names of grandchildren unless the grandparent specifically requested it. It was my way of honoring the privacy of the children and youths who were not interviewed or asked. I followed the same way regarding my own grandchildren and great-grandchildren.

Each of these many people have enriched my awareness of my holy grand-parent vocation. My hope is that this book will do the same for you and will be a tool for you to talk about it with others. Enjoy and God bless your every relationship!

Introduction

Consider a Possibility—Grandparent as a Calling, a Vocation

"The idea that no one is perfect is a view most commonly held by people with no grandchildren."

—Doug Larson[1]

"Grandchildren are the crown of the aged, And the glory of children is their parents."

—Proverbs 17:6

"Congratulations! You have just left the old age of youth and entered the youth of old age." I first saw this on a card sent to me on my fiftieth birthday.

To my delight, I discovered that this saying was true for me. Though I had always thought of fifty as old, I was glad to experience my fifties as remarkably young. I felt good, jogged regularly, played vigorous pickup basketball, and was enrolled in a program to upgrade my pastoral counseling credentials. Fifty was younger than I thought.

Except for one thing. At about the same time, my daughter Julie and son-in-law John told us they were expecting their first child. I was happy for them but chagrined for me! I may have felt young, but "grandfather" felt old! (I don't entirely understand my resistance. After all, fifty is a quite average time for grandparenting to begin.)

By contrast, my wife, Mary Ann, a few years younger than me, was perfectly relaxed and happy with the news of this impending birth. She began thinking about what we could do for them. She saw a simple and colorful

1

baby quilt in a store window, drew a sketch of it, and started making one for the baby.

Months later, their healthy baby boy was born—the first boy in the family since me. Mary Ann had traveled the hundreds of miles to be with them for the birth and to help with care in the first weeks. I had stayed behind and worked. He was given my name for his middle name. (I was honored, but it occurred to me that he would only hear my name when he was in trouble!) I was happy and excited at this news, and my resistance was at least beginning to crumble.

I saw my grandson for the first time about a month later, when we met halfway in between our homes at my mother's, which was near Mary Ann's grandmother. We wanted to be sure to get some five-generation pictures, and the great- and great-great-grandmas were in frail condition.

To say I was drawn to him like a magnet is to put it too tamely! My remaining resistance vanished instantly! For those few days, whenever it was allowed, I was with him: holding him, talking to him, studying his expressions. Someone said we were bonding, but we did not need that—we were bonded! I crumpled with sadness when, at the end of the weekend, we had to go our separate ways.

And so began the adventure of grandparenting for me. At age four or so, he told his mother that he and I were "best buddies." I have received a few other recognitions and awards in my life, but none of them made me any happier!

He was joined by five more—two sisters and three cousins, each of them greatly loved and enjoyed. These six are now in their twenties and thirties. Those birth and childhood gatherings have developed into longer journeys of learning, growing, sometimes struggling, and achieving. Marriages have happened and great-grandchildren are now appearing!

After I got over my resistance, I came to realize that grandparenting brings a whole new dimension. Life is bigger and vaster; our horizons grow. New visions, concerns, and tasks summon us. Little did I realize how enriched I would be by these relationships, nor did I know how my concerns would expand!

Now, "grandparent" is one of my key self-identifiers. Who I am, where I want to be, what I am committed to—all of this arises in large part from my love for my grandchildren, my great-grandchildren, and their contemporaries. It impacts not only who I am but what I do.

A word for this new situation, this grandparent consciousness, may be *calling* or *vocation*. In this book, I will suggest to you that grandparenting may indeed be one's Christian vocation for this season of life, or at least a vital part of it. This is a calling to be the best we can be and to offer the finest within us to our grandchildren. And it is more. In this book I will explore various opportunities to take part in this vocation.

For the last couple of years, I have been on this journey of discovery and reflection on grandparenting as a Christian vocation. I began with my own and Mary Ann's passion, love, and investment in our grandchildren. I also turned to others, including interviews with some two dozen grandparents and a few grandchildren, along with many informal conversations and discussion groups. I am also grounded by about forty years as pastor in churches with intergenerational families.

I read widely—grandparent reflections as well as explorations of what is happening in recent history, in the newer generations, and in religion and society. This investigation included several races, ethnic groups, and nationalities; a spectrum of Christian believers; and a variety of economic situations.

And now I invite you into that journey of discovery.

Here is the conversation I propose.

In chapter 1, I will examine the biblical perspective. What does the Bible say about grandparenting, directly and indirectly? And what does it tell us about vocation?

Chapter 2 invites a look at our varied experiences of being initiated into this vocation, this sorority/fraternity of grandparenting. What are the elements of this initiation? How does it bring us closer to our grandchildren and to each other?

In chapter 3, there is a pause for perspective on grandparenting. The last century and a half have brought vast changes to aging, to birth rates, to who grandparents are, and to their opportunities and limitations. There are also some uncertainties about grandparenting. All of this is good to know as we grow into these relationships.

Chapter 4 describes some of the variety of ways of being grandparents, of living out our calling. What do our grandchildren and family need from us, and how urgent are these needs? What roles will we play in the family? What interests, skills, hobbies, commitments, or causes can we share with our grandchildren? How does this come together into what kind of grandparents we will be?

In chapter 5, I explore a favorite subject—celebration, laughter, and play with our grandchildren. These moments are to be treasured and expanded!

In chapter 6 there is exploration of grandparenting through our grandchildren's years and ours. This is growth to be celebrated and supported as our grandchildren grow and age. There are also hazards of many kinds that they may encounter. During these years, we grandparents are also aging and changing.

In chapter 7, we consider that other people's grandkids may need a lift from us as well. This also may be part of our calling. There may be volunteer activities that beckon us, even if we are far away from our own grandchildren, hoping someone will do the same for them.

In chapter 8, attention is given to grandparents who have the parenting of grandchildren thrust upon them. It is important to know who they are, how they arrive at this place, and what are their biggest issues and needs. These grandparents-as-parents may need our support.

In chapter 9, we consider that our love for our grandchildren may stir a concern for our fragile planet. We hope that this "good earth," God's creation, will be safe and supportive for them—and *their* children and grandchildren. Discussion, projects, activities, and more on intergenerational care for our planet will be offered.

In chapter 10, I will explore communicating about our faith and values. The last sixty years have seen vast changes in religious involvement and in beliefs, values, and ethics. Grandparents, parents, and grandchildren may share a common faith and practice, or there may be huge differences between them. Furthermore, political differences have hardened and polarized. Families may be spread across the vast spectrum of these differences. Our grandparent love and vocation guides us to witness, living out our faith and offering respectful dialogue across the generations and the differences.

In chapter 11, I invite you to consider that as part of our calling, we offer a legacy. When people speak of leaving a legacy, they often are thinking of finances or property, perhaps objects of extrinsic or intrinsic value. That is fine, but there are other legacies that can be offered as well—family stories and identity, faith heritage, rich experiences, and loving relationships, for example. Grandparents may have one more legacy to offer: faith-filled peace when facing the end of life.

In chapter 12, we consider that older people are often much happier than others imagine. One of the sources of that happiness can be family, including grandchildren and great-grandchildren. These grandchildren are a part of how our life, faith, and witness will go on after we are no longer alive. Caring about them, communicating with them, praying for them—this can be an enriching part of the grandparent's spiritual journey.

In a brief postscript, I note that there will come a time to live out another part of the grandparent vocation: frail grandparenthood. While we may have less to give, it can be a time of being, learning to receive as gift, accepting, trying to live with a minimum of demanding, but also praying and committing. We can hope for a good conclusion to our life and our grandparent pilgrimage.

I enjoy and learn from stories, and so there are many on these pages—my own, those of people with whom I visited, and those I have read.

This can be an individual read. It can also be a resource for discussions, book reading groups, Sunday school classes, and more. To help with this, there are some questions for personal or group reflection at the end of each chapter.

I hope that my conversation with in you in this book broadens your grandparent vision and expands to others in one-on-one conversations or larger grandparent groups as you reflect, laugh, and discover together.

So welcome! Let the adventurous conversations begin.

FOR GROUP OR PERSONAL REFLECTION

1. What memories about your grandparenting does this chapter stir? How does your journey into grandparenting compare with mine? (If you are meeting as a group, certainly it will be permissible to bring a few pictures.)
2. I have spoken about how grandparenting changed me. How has it changed you?
3. On a scale of 1 (unaware or unconvinced) to 10 (wildly enthusiastic), where were you in your thinking about grandparenting as a Christian vocation before you read this chapter? Where are you now?
4. Of the topics I have suggested, which do you eagerly anticipate? Which, if any, do you dread? What have I missed or left out? What does the vocation of grandparenting mean to you?
5. Who are some people with whom you would like to talk about grandparenting?

NOTE

1. Doug Larson, quoted in Lesley Stahl, *Becoming Grandma: The Joys and Science of the New Grandparenting* (New York: Blue Rider Press, 2016), 113.

Chapter 1

Biblical Perspectives on the Grandparent Vocation

"But the steadfast love of God is from everlasting to everlasting on those who revere God, and God's righteousness to children's children, to those who keep the covenant and remember to do God's commandments."

—Psalm 103:17–18, An Inclusive Version

"Perfect love sometimes does not come until the first grandchild."

—Welsh Proverb[1]

As I consider that being a grandparent is not only a delight but also a Christian vocation, I turn to the Bible for insight and guidance. As one of my Bible teachers pointed out, the Bible *is* the Word of God, *contains* the Word of God, and *becomes* the Word of God, as we participate in conversation with its texts and with each other.

The Bible contains the stories of God engaging God's people. It also includes God's basic commandments for living in covenant with God and with each other. Further, the Bible tells of the prophets who call people back to justice and right living. And further still, the Bible contains wisdom, with practical insights for good living.

The Bible brings us the story of the birth, life, teachings, death, and resurrection of Jesus. It also includes the story of the early church and the guidance provided it and us on how to live as Jesus's followers. It is a rich library of sixty-six books, this Bible of ours!

Granted, the Bible was not written specifically as a manual for grandparents. Still, we can look within our Bible for insights and guidance about the grandparent vocation. These will be found within this larger narrative. There is much that we will find. In the following pages, I will tell you what I discovered as I carried on this search.

GRANDCHILDREN AS RARE AND WONDERFUL GIFT

To begin, I learned that life expectancy was such that fewer would get to be grandparents and that the length of time with grandchildren might be quite limited. Possibly, this will take us by surprise. We might think of the 90th Psalm, "The days of our life are seventy years, perhaps eighty, if we are strong" (v. 10), much less the earlier mention of the life span of Methuselah (Gen. 5:25–27) and others.

However, in the 90th Psalm, the psalmist was speaking of the rare and fortunate individuals who lived that long. Earlier verses in this psalm speak of the shortness of life: "You sweep them away, they are like a dream, like grass that is renewed in the morning; in the morning it flourishes and is renewed; in the evening it fades and withers" (v. 5–6).

In his book *Cultural Dictionary of the Bible*, Bible scholar John Pilch points out that study of skeletal remains reveal that life expectancy in the ancient world probably averaged in the range of thirty to forty-five years. This archeological work also reveals that almost 30 percent of children died before they reached the age of six. Another 60 percent died before their mid-teens and 75 percent before their mid-twenties. Only 10 percent likely made it to their mid-forties, and possibly as few as 3 percent to their sixties![2] Pilch further points out that as startling as this may seem, safe childbirth and healthy childhood are quite recent developments. At the beginning of the twentieth century, a woman had to bear 6.1 children just to replace herself. Smallpox and diphtheria, among others, were common, lethal childhood diseases.

Of course, people married and bore children at much younger ages then than they do now—for young women, often in their early or mid-teens. Grandparenthood came at a younger time as well. Still, with all the hazards—and fragility—of life, for both the child and the adult, grandparenthood was experienced as a rare and wonderful gift, not nearly as widespread or lengthy as now.

Indeed, there are Bible passages that celebrate grandchildren as a special gift of God and pray that gift for others. For example, Proverbs 17:6: "Grandchildren are the crown of the aged, and the glory of children is their parents." There is also the prayer/blessing found in Psalm 128:5–6: "The Lord bless you from Zion. May you see the prosperity of Jerusalem. May you see your children's children. Peace be upon Israel!" For those of us who live in the twenty-first century, with increased life expectancies for us and our grandchildren, these verses guide us into even deeper gratitude and joy and awareness of the trust given us.

There is also word about mutual care and provision across the generations. For example, in Proverbs 13:22, we are told, "The good leave an inheritance to their children's children." On the other hand, guidance offered in 1 Timothy about care in the New Testament church community counsels: "If a widow has children or grandchildren, they should first learn their religious duty to their own family and make some repayment to their parents; for this is pleasing in God's sight" (1 Tim. 5:4).

A FOUNDATIONAL TEACHING
ABOUT GRANDPARENTS

While the focus of this book is the calling and responsibility *of* grandparents, scholars point to one foundational passage of responsibility *to* grandparents. It is Exodus 20:12, the fifth commandment: "Honor your father and your mother, so that your days may be long in the land that the LORD your God is giving you."

This is given in the pivotal spot between the first four commandments, which speak of human relationships with God, and the last five, which address human relationships with each other. Clearly it is addressed not to children about their parents, but to adults about their aging parents.

To *honor* means to give weight, to acknowledge the worth and importance of a person. It may even mean to revere the person.

Part of honoring parents meant giving financial and economic support. Ronald Clements notes, "When families lived together in large groups, aging parents who could no longer work were entirely dependent upon their children to support them economically. It is this care of the old that is demanded [in this commandment]."[3]

In action, honoring a grandparent is multifaceted. As Josh Mulvill summarizes, this honoring "is demonstrated by positive actions in their behalf—meeting their needs, listening to their advice, recognizing their worth, and doing so in all sorts of ways large and small."[4]

This foundational Bible passage reminds us that grandparent-grandchild joy is a two-way street, with responsibilities and gifts each for the other.

INCIDENTAL MENTIONING OF
GRANDPARENTS OR GRANDCHILDREN

There are also times when grandchildren or grandparents are mentioned incidentally as a part of some other story. For example, in Exodus 10:2, God tells Moses to speak to Pharoah, whose heart is hardened, "that you may tell your children and grandchildren how I have made fools of the Egyptians and what signs I have done among them—so you may know that I am the LORD."

Another incidental mention—In 2 Samuel 9, there is the story of King David's generosity to Mephibosheth, his late dearest friend Jonathan's son. In part of the story David speaks to the young man: "Do not be afraid, for I will show you kindness for the sake of your father Jonathan; I restore to you all the land of your grandfather Saul, and you yourself shall eat at my table always" (2 Sam. 9:7).

In 1 Chronicles 8:40, there is note of a remarkably hardy family: "The sons of Ulam were mighty warriors, archers, having many children and grandchildren, one hundred fifty. All these were Benjaminites."

These are events where grandchildren and grandparents are mentioned but are not the center of focus or teaching.

GRANDMOTHER STORIES

Athaliah

There are at least three grandmother stories in the Bible. One of these, Athaliah, is not at all pleasant. In 2 Kings 11:1 we are told, "Now when Athaliah the mother of Ahaziah saw that her son was dead, she arose and destroyed all the royal family." Athaliah, the daughter of King Ahab and the notorious Jezebel, assassinated the king's children and grandchildren, anyone who might have claim on the throne of Judah, so that she might be ruling queen herself! Raymond Calkins notes, "Athaliah thus stands out in history as the incarnation of cruelty, a masterful conscience-less nature, capable of swift resolution, relentless purpose, devoid of any instinct either of natural affection or of common humanity."[5] This is not the way we usually think of a grandmother!

And so she set out to assassinate sons and grandsons, anyone with a claim to the throne, so that it could be hers alone to occupy. However, the late king's sister Jehosheba (wife of the priest Jehoiada) took the late king's infant son, Joash, and "stole him away from among the king's children who were about to be killed; she put him and his nurse in a bedroom . . . so that he was not killed; he remained with her six years, hidden in the house of the LORD, while Athaliah ruled over the land" (2 Kings 11:2b–3).

And so Athaliah ruled for six years. In the seventh, the priest Jehoiada staged a coup d'état on a sabbath. He did so while the temple guard was being changed. Athaliah was killed and seven-year-old Joash was placed on the throne and crowned king!

This part of the story concludes with the opening verses of 2 Kings 12: "In the seventh year of Jehu, Jehoash [another form of the name Joash] began to reign; he reigned forty years in Jerusalem. His mother's name was Zibiah of Beersheba. Jehoash did what was right in the sight of the Lord all his days, because the priest Jehoiada instructed him" (v. 1–2).

Biological grandparenthood, by itself, confers no virtues! Becoming grandparent may be a summons to become a better person, an invitation into a journey of discovery, growth, and especially love. Or, as this cautionary tale warns, grandparenthood may not change us from our selfish ways.

Naomi

In the little book of Ruth is the story of an unlikely grandmother, Naomi. Her name means "my joy" or "pleasant," but by the midpoint of the story, she understandably tells her neighbors, "Call me no longer Naomi, call me Mara" (that is, "bitter"; Ruth 2:10b). She and her husband, Elimelech, along with their two sons, Mahlon and Chilion, had left their home country of Judah due to famine. They traveled to the neighboring country of Moab, a country historically their enemy, a people Israelites thought of as lacking virtue. Indeed, " Moab in the Hebrew Scriptures is constructed as enduringly carnal, sexual, deviant."[6]

While there, their two sons married Moabite women. (Certainly, women from their own tribe and home country would have been preferred.) Then her husband died; her two sons also died, both without leaving any children behind. Naomi concluded there was nothing for her in Moab and decided to return to her home, Bethlehem in Judah.

Her daughters-in-law chose to go back with her, but she discouraged them, telling them she would have no more sons for them to marry. The Bible account records, "Then they wept aloud. Orpah kissed her mother-in-law [goodbye], but Ruth clung to her" (Ruth 1:14).

When Naomi again urged Ruth to return to her own people, she responded with words so often remembered and treasured: "Do not press me to leave you or to turn back from following you! Where you go, I will go; where you lodge, I will lodge; your people shall be my people and your God my God. Where you die, I will die—there will I be buried" (Ruth 1:16–17a). However, Kat Armas points out that this statement should not be romanticized. Both women had lost their husbands, thus both their financial support and their protection. Ruth's statement "is a simple commitment rooted in survival."[7]

And so they went together to Bethlehem. They arrived in Bethlehem at the beginning of the barley harvest. For their provision, Ruth went to the fields to glean whatever was left by the harvesting crews, a hazardous and risky task for a lone woman. She wound up gleaning in the fields of Boaz, who was a kinsman of Naomi from her husband's family. In time, Boaz was impressed with Ruth's industry and faithfulness. Naomi then "devise[d] a second plan, more cunning and clever than the first. Naomi encourage[d] Ruth to dress up, put on perfume, wait till Boaz is drunk, then sneak into his bedroom and seduce him."[8] In a hazardous world, Naomi helped them survive by being a trickster who "has to employ wit and cunning to achieve the desired end."[9]

Eventually, there was some delicate negotiation with another kinsman about purchasing the dead kinsman's land and accepting responsibility for his widow and providing progeny.

In time, "Boaz took Ruth, and she became his wife" (Ruth 4:13). She conceived and had a baby boy. After all the hardships of Ruth and Naomi, this was a time of great celebration. For one thing, with the arrival of this little boy, "Mara" became "Naomi" again—bitter became sweet.

The women of the village spoke to Naomi, "Blessed be the LORD who has not left you this day without next-of-kin; and may his name be renowned in Israel! He shall be to you a restorer of life and a nourisher of your old age; for your daughter-in-law who loves you, who is more to you than seven sons, has borne him" (Ruth 4:14–15). He was named Obed.

Strictly speaking, Obed was not Naomi's biological grandson. However, he was a grandchild by the rules of levirate marriage, in which a kinsman of a dead person who was childless married the widow, and if a child was born, it became the dead person's heir. Still, from time immemorial, exact biological grandparenthood was never a requirement for loving and cherishing the newborn member of a new generation!

And so Grandma Naomi "took the child and laid him on her bosom and became his nurse" (Ruth 4:16). Grandmother and mother did well. When he grew up, Obed was the father of Jesse, and years later, Jesse was the father of the great king David—Ruth's great-grandchild and Naomi's great-great-grandchild.

Lois

This grandmother story is offered in one tantalizing Bible verse—2 Timothy 1:5: "I am reminded of your sincere faith, a faith that lived first in your grandmother Lois and your mother Eunice, and now, I am sure, lives in you."

Kat Armas tells of the powerful impact of this verse on her. She writes,

By acknowledging Timothy's faith (a faith birthed from his abuelita [beloved grandmother] and his mama), Paul honors the two women, puts their names in ink, so that they are forever remembered—canonized if you will. He acknowledges that their faith is a communal faith that takes seriously the impact of not just the people who came before him, but the *women* who formed and shaped him. That powerful affirmation has changed the course of my life.[10]

We would love to know more, but this verse is all that we have. Timothy's mother is mentioned—but not by name—in Acts 16, where we first meet him. In the apostle Paul's travels, he came to Lystra, where he met Timothy, described as a disciple, well-spoken of by the believers in Lystra. The passage says Timothy was "the son of a Jewish woman who was a believer, but his father was a Greek" (Acts 16:1b). At that point, there is no mention of his grandmother.

This, then, is all we know about Lois. I do not know about you, but if there could be only one sentence to describe my life and it said that my faithful witness has endured to a third generation, where it is being embraced, renewed, and lived—that would be enough!

OTHER BIBLE THEMES OF IMPORTANCE FOR GRANDPARENTS

Generations: Grandparenting by Another Name

Another way the Bible speaks of grandparenting is with the frequent mention of *generations* in the Bible. Of course, generations refer to our contemporaries, our children, their children, and so on down the line; in other words, grandparenthood many times over.

In the Bible there is also word of the generations who came before us. For example, in Exodus 3, as God is calling Moses to lead the children of Israel out of Egypt, God tells Moses to say, "The God of your ancestors, the God of Abraham, the God of Isaac, and the God of Jacob has sent me to you." (Exod. 3:15). In other words, the God of your great grandfathers, several times over, is acting again on your behalf.

The Bible refers again and again to God's promises as regards future generations. For example, in Genesis 9, after the flood, God places the rainbow in the heavens and tells Noah, "This is the sign of the covenant I make between me and you and every living creature that is with you, for all future generations" (Gen. 9:12). Later, God covenants with Abraham, "I will establish my covenant between me and you, and your offspring after you throughout their generations for an everlasting covenant to be God to you and to your offspring after you" (Gen. 17: 7).

The Bible makes clear that God's covenant with us is an enduring relationship. In Exodus 20:6, within the Ten Commandments God describes Godself as "showing steadfast love to the thousandth generation of those who love me and keep my commandments." The thousandth generation! This is a promise that is repeated; see, for example, Deuteronomy 7:9, 1 Chronicles 16:15, and Psalm 105.8.

This mention of generations continues in the New Testament. For example, in Mary's song of praise, she states, "His mercy is for those who fear him from generation to generation" (Luke 1:50). And in the letter to the Ephesians, there is the word "to him be glory in the church and in Christ Jesus to all generations forever and ever amen" (Eph. 3:20–21).

While God promises care to generations unending, there is also the responsibility for the elders to communicate this faith heritage and teach it to the generations after them. And there are ways provided to do this. For example, the Passover celebration is to be observed each year to remember God's deliverance from bondage in Egypt: "This shall be a day of remembrance for you. You shall celebrate it as a festival to the LORD; throughout your generations you shall observe it as a perpetual ordinance" (Exod. 12:14).

Later there is the appointment of Aaron and his sons as priests to uphold these teachings and traditions, "and their anointing shall admit them to a perpetual priesthood throughout all generations to come" (Exod. 40:15). Today's grandparents will also do well to ask how we can use the holidays and practices of our faith to communicate our faith story and our commitment to our grandchildren and theirs.

In addition to their practices such as Passover, priesthood, and sabbath, elders are to tell the story of their people's deliverance in song, word, and story. For example, Psalm 145:4: "One generation shall laud your works to another, and shall declare your mighty acts," or Psalm 78:4: "We will not hide them from our children; we will tell to the coming generation the glorious deeds of the LORD and his might, and the wonders that he has done." The psalmist continues, "He established a decree in Jacob and appointed a law in Israel, which he commanded our ancestors to teach to their children that the next generation might know them, the children yet unborn, and rise up and tell them to their children so that they should set their hope in God and not forget the works of God" (Ps. 78:5–6).

In obedience, one psalmist prays, "So even to old age and gray hairs, O God, do not forsake me until I proclaim your might to all the generations to come" (Ps 71:18).

Persons are to tell generations the historic deliverance of their people. Not only that, they are called to share about their own personal encounters with God, and God's response to their pain and need. In Psalm 22, there is divine response to a person's desperate personal prayer. As this psalmist praises God for this response, they[11] make this promise: "Posterity will serve him; future generations will be told about the Lord, and proclaim his deliverance to a people yet unborn, saying that he has done it" (Ps. 22:31).

Generations, hundreds of them, are to tell of the heritage of their faith to the generations after them and to model faithful obedience to God and relationship with God for them. Grandparents are needed in case parents forget!

Jesus and Children

Another biblical resource for grandparents is Jesus's relationships with children. He lived in an age where there was little attention paid to childhood per se and children were expected to grow quickly into their working lives and adult duties. In this setting, Jesus's frequent attention to and care with children is even more surprising.

In Mark 9 and 10, three revealing vignettes are offered close together. In Mark 9:33–37, Jesus confronts his disciples' argument about who was the greatest. He first speaks to them about being servants to each other: "Then he took a little child and put it among them; and taking it in his arms, he said to them, 'Whoever welcomes one such child in my name welcomes me, and whoever welcomes me welcomes not me but the one who sent me.'" Welcome a child as you would welcome Jesus!

Matthew relates this incident from a slightly different perspective and includes a further word from Jesus; when asked who is greatest in God's kingdom, "he called a child, whom he put among them and said, 'Truly I tell you, unless you change and become like children, you will never enter the kingdom of heaven. Whoever becomes humble like this child is the greatest in the kingdom of heaven'" (Matt. 18:3–4). Listen and observe children carefully. In many ways, including their curiosity, openness, teachableness—humility—children have so much to teach us. Susan Lebel Young has written a book about what her grandchildren have taught her. She titled it *Grandkids as Gurus*.[12] In the light of his verse, Jesus would certainly have concurred.

But children's lives and faith are just forming; this faith is fragile and can be crushed by neglect, inconsistency, conflicts/fights, harshness, or insensitivity. It is wise to heed Jesus's solemn word: "If any of you put a stumbling block before one of these little ones who believe in me, it would be better for you if a great millstone were hung around your neck and you were thrown into the sea." (Mark 9:42). That is God's child entrusted to you, and you are responsible to God for the child's faith and learning. Handle with care![13]

Then there is the incident in Mark 10:13–16 (and other gospels). Parents who loved their children came simply requesting that Jesus touch them! However, the disciples "spoke sternly to them." This appears callous. However, perhaps we should not judge them too harshly. This event is described in a tense time near the end of Jesus's ministry. He had spoken at least twice of his coming persecution and death in Jerusalem, and they were approaching Jerusalem. The disciples may have been trying to save Jesus from more stress.

However, he would have none of it. Tired, sad, and stressed as he might have been, Jesus "was indignant": "Let the children come to me; do not stop them; for it is to such as these that the kingdom of God belongs." Then, as Mark vividly describes it, beyond the simple touch the parents requested, "he took them up in his arms, laid his hands on them, and blessed them."

As Jesus welcomed the children, do you imagine he might have winked at them, tickled them, played a little game, or told them a story or two? Certainly, this picture of a tired and stressed Jesus making generous time for children has importance for all of us who have children entrusted to our care.

Earlier in this chapter I mentioned the frailty and high mortality rate of children in biblical times. Considering this, it is important to note how often Jesus responded to fearful parents and healed their children, as mentioned in Mark 7:24–30, Luke 8:40–55, and John 4:46–50. He wanted children cured, safe, healthy, alive, and restored to their parents' loving care.

In the gospels we meet Jesus as lover, respecter, and advocate for children. Jesus bids followers, including grandparents, to offer corresponding love and care. Jesus's teaching and example about children affirms something we are already eager to do.

Vocation

There is one other biblical topic that is important to us as grandparents. That is the subject of vocation. While the word *vocation* has been used mostly to designate one's occupation, it has a more basic meaning: It comes from the Latin word *voco* which means "to call" or "to summon."

The Bible speaks of many calls. In the Hebrew Bible (Old Testament), God calls Israel to be the people of God. And then God calls persons to carry out tasks within this people—prophets, priests, leaders. In the New Testament, Jesus calls people to repentance and then calls certain persons to be his disciples and apostles. All are called of God, some to specific tasks and responsibilities.

From this perspective, the concept of vocation speaks to our Christian life throughout our days. The old hymn "Jesus Calls Us" captures this under-standing. We are led to ask, to what are we called in each chapter of our lives? As we ponder this, we may find insight in a tantalizing passage in the New Testament. In 1 Corinthians 7:17–31, the apostle Paul offers guidance to persons in the various circumstances of their life. His first word in this regard, is verse 17: "Let each of you lead the life that the Lord has assigned, to which

God called you." He speaks of such life circumstances as being circumcised according to Jewish custom, employment (including, in this setting, slavery), and marriage or singleness. In verse 20, he comes back to one's calling. As the King James Version accurately translates, what Paul said was, "Let every [person] abide in *the same calling* wherein [that person] was *called*" [emphasis mine]. In other words, you were called to faith in God through Christ, but you were also called to be where you are and do what you do.

I acknowledge that this passage needs to be interpreted carefully. I do not read it that God specifically willed or called persons to be circumcised or not, slaves or not, married or not, but that God's call is to be faithful from whatever state one is in. Likewise, there are some who would love to have grandchildren, but none come to their family. And there are those who would love to have more access to their grandchildren but are limited by family conflict or divorce settlements. In each of these situations, we are called to be faithful and caring whether we would have chosen that circumstance or not.

At the same time, I have become aware of the great Christian leader Howard Thurman's reflection about reading scripture to his grandmother, Nancy Ambrose. She was born into slavery and could not read or write. Grandmother Nancy was very clear what scripture he could and could not read to her, and she wanted little or none of Paul's epistles. Why? Because in slavery, the master's minister would preach to the slaves and at least four times a year would preach on Colossians 3:22, "Slaves be obedient to them that are your masters . . . as unto Christ." His grandmother told him, "*I promised my Maker that if I ever learned to read and if freedom ever came, I would not read that part of the Bible.*"[14]

Thurman and his grandmother might have objected to this passage as well. With or without this Corinthian text, the Bible does speak of our callings, our vocation. Throughout this book I will explore all that God's call implies for our lives as grandparents.

To begin, within this calling/vocation to be Christ's follower, there is much guidance as to how to treat each other and how to live together in Christian community. For example, Ephesians 4:32: "And be kind to one another, tenderhearted, forgiving one another as God in Christ has forgiven you." As we offer such care to fellow believers, we would certainly also extend it—even more so—to our own grandchildren!

Additionally, as Josh Mulvihill notes, the Bible teaches "grandparents are expected to supply a rich Christian heritage for their grandchildren" in its many dimensions.[15]

And so, in addition to our occupation—and after we may have retired from an occupation—what other vocations/callings await us? Just possibly, could grandchildren be that vocation, that calling for us, or at very least, an important part of our vocation? Did you feel a profound stirring, a life shift, when a grandchild was born (or adopted or otherwise welcomed into your family)? If so, to what does that deep affection, that unbounded love, call you? Where might such a calling lead? That is what we will explore together in the following chapters.

FOR GROUP CONVERSATION OR PERSONAL REFLECTION

1. Do you know any grandparents who are "Loises"—whose faith and witness has impacted the generations after them? What can you tell about them and what they offered? Are you such a person? If so, what have been the ways you achieved this?
2. As you think about what the Bible says about grandparenthood, what would you add to this chapter? What did it leave out?
3. What, if anything, in this chapter surprised you? With what, if anything, in this chapter did you disagree or have serious questions?
4. As you reflect on Jesus's interaction with and care for children, what specifically does this say to you as a grandparent?
5. What Bible passage speaks most deeply to you about your calling as grandparent? What are your fondest hopes about your grandparent vocation/calling? About your faith journey with your grandchildren?

NOTES

1. Quoted in Richard Eyre, *Being a Proactive Grandfather: How to Make a Difference* (New York: Familius, 2017), 4.

2. John Pilch, *The Cultural Dictionary of the Bible* (Collegeville, MN: Liturgical Press, 1999), 145.

3. Stephen Sapp, *Full of Years: Aging and the Elderly in the Bible and Today* (Nashville: Abingdon Press, 1987), 82. He is quoting Ronald E. Clements.

4. Josh Mulvihill, *Biblical Grandparenting: Exploring God's Design for Disciple-Making and Passing Faith to Future Generations* (Minneapolis: Bethany House, 2018), 80.

5. Raymond Calkins, "Exposition of II Kings," *The Interpreter's Bible*, vol. 3 (New York: Abingdon Press, 1954), 245.

6. Kat Armas, *Abuelita Faith: What Women on the Margins Teach Us about Wisdom, Persistence, and Strength* (Grand Rapids, MI: Brazos Press, 2021), 103. She, in turn, is summarizing the views of Yolanda Norton.

7. Armas, *Abeuelita Faith*, 104.

8. Armas, *Abeuelita Faith*, 106.

9. Armas, *Abeuelita Faith,* 107.

10. Armas, *Abeuelita Faith,* 34.

11. Here "they" is used as a third-person singular pronoun.

12. Susan Lebel Young, *Grandkids as Gurus: Lessons for Adults* (Just Write Press, 2020).

13. I acknowledge that some Bible scholars believe this saying is not about children, but perhaps rather about the weak in faith or those without wealth or position or learning. I choose to believe that in this setting, Jesus is cautioning and guiding about the spiritual care of children.

14. Yolanda Pierce, *In My Grandmother's House: Black Women, Faith, and the Stories We Inherit* (Minneapolis: Broadleaf Press, 2021), 123–24. She is quoting Howard Thurman, *Jesus and the Disinherited*; italics theirs.

15. Mulvihill, *Biblical Grandparenting,* 129.

Chapter 2

The Grandparent's Initiation—
The Grandparent's Call

"Young men and women alike, old and young together!"

—Psalm 148:12

"The grandparent/grandchild relationship may be the purest relationship that we humans have."

—Mary Pipher[1]

TWO QUESTIONS

One, what is a grandparent? We think we know, but what is a grandparent in all its dimensions? Is it a role or a collection of roles? A status? A relationship? An emotion? Is it a responsibility? An invitation? An openness? A perspective? A calling? Is it all of these, and perhaps more?

Two, how does one become a grandparent? Of course, this happens when one's biological child becomes the parent of their biological child. But what are the other ways in which "grandparent" occurs?

In this chapter we will explore a variety of initiations into becoming a grandparent. We will also ask what this experience says to us—calls to us. The rest of the book will follow where this leads.

GRANDPARENTING THROUGH A
BIRTH TO ONE'S CHILD

For many, grandparenting begins when a child is born to your child. This is how it happened for Mary Ann and me. I told a bit about our experience in the introduction. For Mary Ann, the excitement began when the pregnancy was announced—anticipating, preparing, making a gift.

For me, my initial resistance ended, mostly, with the birth. I heard the news from a distance; I was not present because of my work. But the exciting news of a new grandchild entered into my consciousness and my conversation with everyone I saw those days. I remember being with an elderly women's Bible study I led. They knew the child was coming. When I told them he had been born, Helen, one of the group members, said to me, "Dick, now you are going to discover what love really is!" In a very short time, I would discover how true Helen's words were.

I was indeed overwhelmed with that love when I saw him for the first time a month later. This was an ecstasy akin to when each of our three children were born, but also something more, something different. The horizons grew even more; my world expanded. I measured time from when I last saw him to when I could see him next. (I was fully employed at the time, and we lived hundreds of miles apart.) Each subsequent grandchild's birth further warmed my world and brightened my future.

Lesley Stahl, a journalist with *60 Minutes*, reflects similarly on the birth of her granddaughter: "Becoming grandmother turns the page. Line by line you are rewritten. You are tilted off your old center, spun into new turf. . . . Here you rediscover fun and laughing and reach a depth of pure loving you have never felt before. . . . [It] exhilarated me with new purpose. The change was so big and granular and unexpected."[2]

She recalls being present at the birth: "I was so pumped, my heart was on a trampoline. . . . When it was my turn [to hold the new baby] I felt I was growing a whole new chamber in my heart. I nearly swooned, staring at her like a lover. I'd never seen anything so delicate and beautiful, so sweet, every feature perfect. . . . I was overwhelmed with euphoria."[3]

Her excitement about her new grandchild continued when they were separated from each other. She recalls being in bed, pretending she was holding the baby. She recalls, "I was infatuated. Dare I say it? It felt like—ardor."

As she attempted to understand this constant and frequent longing, she contacted Louann Brizendine, author of *The Female Brain*. Brizendine explained that the brain pathway for baby love is the same as the pathway for romantic and carnal love, but the baby brain circuitry came first. Sex later piggybacked on it. Further, just as happens with a new mother, when a grandmother holds a new grandbaby, her brain can be flooded with the bonding hormone oxytocin. Stahl concludes, "Aha! There it was. We grandmas literally, actually, fall in love."[4]

She notes how she and her husband varied in their grandparent response: "Aaron and I were both changed by becoming grandparents but in different ways. I was a jitterbug, he was a waltz; I was electrified, he was softened. We'd be with Jordan together, doing the same things with her, having different experiences. His loving her was every bit as deep as mine. His eyes would well up. But he told me he didn't feel that physical rush, the efflorescence of igniting spark plugs."[5]

Of course, not all grandparents have as an ecstatic first experience with their grandchild. As Kathleen Stassen Berger notes, "instant adoration" eludes some grandparents—and some parents. She notes that delayed bonding may be related to various circumstances of the pregnancy, perhaps drugs at birth, hospital procedures, or attitudes in the culture or the parents. She concludes, "But no matter what the reason, birth is a starting bell: grandmothers need to get ready for the next lesson."[6]

GRANDPARENTING THROUGH ADOPTION

People also become grandparents through adoption.When an adopted child enters a family, there have been many steps and probably years of waiting for and wanting that child to arrive! A couple (or a single person, for that matter) may have very much wanted to conceive and give birth to a child but experienced infertility issues. They may have endured long and costly attempts to become pregnant. Eventually, they concluded that was not going to happen. Or, for various reasons, they may have already known that biological parenting would not occur. Further, there are parents who have biological children and still adopt.

Then they started investigating the adoption process. Whatever path they chose, they needed to demonstrate their readiness. For example, they had to establish that their health was sound enough to care for a child to maturity and that they had no criminal record. They also needed to show that they were financially able to provide for a child and that their home had adequate space for this child.

As a part of this, they made decisions as to what type of adoption to seek and what kind of agency they would engage to guide them through the process. They may have selected a public agency, one with governmental or a religious welfare/social service connection. Or they may have chosen a private agency.

They made a choice whether to seek a domestic adoption (from within their home country) or an international one, and if the latter, from what countries and with what agency. Further, they decided whether they wanted to pursue a closed or open adoption. In a closed adoption, neither the birth parents nor the adoptive parents know who the others are and the two families have no contact. An open adoption is where the birthmother, and sometimes the birth father, and the adoptive parents do know of each other, may meet each other, and may have some sort of contact or involvement after the adoption.[7]

In all of this, there is uncertainty and waiting, certainly for months and probably for years. Further, there is also expense with all kinds of adoptions. On the most basic level, an adoption by a foster family will probably cost a few thousand dollars to cover the various legal processes. A private adoption involves additional expense, contact, and negotiation. Perhaps the expenses of the birth mother may need to be assumed. A recent article suggested the cost for a private adoption might be between $20,000 and $45,000. International adoptions (with fees, travel, and possibly housing and waiting in the country of origin) can run into a significant number of thousands of dollars, estimated at possibly $25,000 to $70,000.[8]

The steps of this process will be varied and are best guided by a good agency or adoption attorney. I visited with our niece Meri Kay and her husband, Trent, and spoke with them about their experience guided by a private adoption attorney. As part of their journey, they initially wrote a "Dear Birth Mother" letter stating why they would like to adopt the child and why they would be a good choice. They promised to provide adequately and that the child would be loved by them and be part of a loving extended family as well as their church, their family of faith. Then they received a call. Based on that letter, they were one of five couples being considered by birth parents and were asked to write a follow-up letter. The birth parents selected them.

In time, they traveled to the hospital where she had given birth, in a different state from where they live, knowing that nothing was certain until she, the birth mother, decided and signed the adoption agreement. The birth mother wavered for a day and even considered taking the baby home for a few days, but then acknowledged that adoption would be for the best. Because of this experience, these adoptive parents are strong advocates for respect and support of birth mothers. They, as well as adoption professionals, urge us never to say a mother "gave up her baby for adoption," but rather "made an adoption plan." This is an important distinction for the adopted child as well.

Once a child is born and the selected adoptive parents have received the child, there are other steps to be taken before the adoption is final. For Meri Kay and Trent, the first step came three days after the birth when the birth mother signed the adoption document. This said she was not under duress and was freely agreeing to grant the adoptive parents custody. They then received the child into their care but could not leave that state with the child for another ten days. Each state has its own laws that apply to all adoptions, whether public or private.

After the waiting period, Meri Kay and Trent then returned to their home with the child, but the adoption was still not final. For the next three months, they were monitored by their state's adoption department.There was paperwork that they were required to provide. There was another visit, where a state worker again inspected the home for fitness, observed them, and interviewed them about their childcare comfort, practices, and provisions.

Meri Kay and Trent remember this as a very tense time. Were they going to be seen as good enough? After all the waiting and uncertainties, they were caring for a child they already loved very much. They did not want to lose him! In retrospect, and for our purposes, they see this as a time when grandparents could be helpful with emotional support during this stressful and uncertain time.

After three months, there was a court hearing. Accompanied by their adoption attorney, Meri Kay and Trent appeared with the baby before a judge in a formal court process. The evaluations and paperwork were reviewed. This judge asked them some very pointed questions: Are you ready for this? Do you accept this responsibility? Are you sure this is the right thing for you? They remember this day as filled with so many emotions. All their reasons for wanting to do this, all their hopes, came down to this moment. After reviewing the documents and hearing their answers, the judge granted the adoption. Then there were moments of gracious informality. As was his custom, the judge had his picture taken with them holding their newly adopted son.

The regulations and duration of this interim period will vary from state to state. In all the steps of adoption, there are many variations of experience. I have been mainly speaking from Meri Kay and Trent's experience of the state in which they live and the state to which they traveled to receive their child.

Grandparents may become involved at any point along this journey. Some parents may not want to subject the potential grandparents to uncertainty and possible disappointment, so they keep the earlier stages to themselves. Others may need emotional and spiritual support from their parents through all the waiting and uncertainty. The adopting parents may also need to ask for financial support, or grandparents may want to stand ready to provide help if needed and if they are able.

The successful conclusion of this journey means that there is a new family member, a child to be welcomed, loved, and cherished! Most grandparents with whom I visited speak with equal ardor and joy of each of their grandchildren, whether they arrived by birth, adoption, or marriage (a child's stepchildren). It just doesn't matter. A grandchild is a grandchild! A few may struggle with disappointment out of hoping for a grandchild to carry on their bloodline. Hopefully bonds will grow so that all are equally loved. (While I have been speaking mostly of the adoption of young children, there are also adoptions of older children and of special needs children as well.)

In my interviews, I heard about all kinds of grandchildren. Some mentioned that at least one of their grandchildren came from China, or Korea, or Russia, or a nation in Africa. I am thinking of one new grandfather who came to tell me of his family's good news. After his daughter's life-threatening surgery and heartbreak attempting to have a child, his daughter and son-in-law had successfully arranged to adopt three little Russian girls, siblings, between three and seven years old. When this man told his best friend of these girls' coming arrival, his friend responded, "So you have three granddaughters you didn't know about until now." His eyes filled—his sentiments exactly. An exciting new set of relationships was beginning!

GRANDPARENTING THROUGH
REFORMULATION OF FAMILIES

Grandchildren come into our lives in yet other ways. For example, it may happen if, after divorce or the death of a spouse, our child remarries, or we do. New relationships are in the offing, waiting to be formed and experienced.

This was the experience of one grandmother, Ann, whom I interviewed. She is the birth grandmother of the three children of one of her sons. Recently, her second son married a woman with children, and they were forging a new family together. Her new daughter-in-law has two children, a girl, fourteen, and a boy, eight, from previous relationships. Then this couple also took in a thirteen-year-old girl, a friend of her daughter's whose father had died and whose family had been unable to provide her a stable home.

And so this grandmother journeyed several hundred miles for a first visit. She went hoping and strategizing how to form relationships with two early teenage girls—with quite different histories and family connections from each other—and with an eight-year-old boy. She was quite aware that these relationships would be based on whatever each young person wanted and was willing to accept. At the same time, she hoped to develop loving bonds with each person in this family her son loved. As it happened, during this visit her daughter-in-law was gone due to a death in the family.

Ann spent the weekend going to volleyball matches, playing games, learning about the children's hobbies and interests (especially the girls' enjoyment of painting and the eight-year-old's love of birds). She braided hair for the girls and joined in family with them for a few days. On the early morning she left, one of the girls had left one of her paintings for Ann. She tells me, "It has a big moon, stars, insects among the grasses. It is a beautiful painting of nature. I am touched that she gave it to me." She came away hopeful that first steps had been taken toward trusting relationships, fulfilling for all.

Kathleen Stassen Berger tells of another grandmother's experience. This woman had two sons, but one had died suddenly at age eighteen. Her other son, Colin, had left home in early adulthood to work a thousand miles away. Three years later, Colin was coming home for Christmas (though his parents, still in mourning for his brother, did not celebrate Christmas). He was bringing the woman he loved, Andrea, and her son, Brandon, with him.

The woman wrote that when they got off the plane, "[Brandon] rolled straight into my arms. I could not believe it. . . . I had a grandson. . . . We didn't count up to figure how many grandmothers a boy needed or deserved. In the end, blood counts, but not as much as love."

This grieving couple had not had a Christmas tree since their son's death, but she thought this was not fair for a child. So she had tied some red ribbons on the branches of a Ficus tree in the living room and put a few wrapped presents under it. This amazed and pleased the young boy, who had been told there would be no tree.

A few days later, the two—the woman and the child—had a serious talk. She explained that Andrea and Colin might marry or not, might break up, but "I would be his grandmother as long as he wanted me to. . . . And we shook on that. And nothing has changed in the last twenty or so years since."

Stassen Berger concludes, "This was a fortunate lifelong relationship that helped the woman recover from bereavement and that sustained Brandon through school and college. Colin and Andrea married, broke up, and then got back together; the grandmother/Brandon relationship continued to anchor the boy through it all."[9]

Another grandparent, David, was delighted with his relationship with his stepdaughter's children, "There's no such thing as a step-grandpa. It doesn't matter how many grandparents you have. To the children, I'm just another grandpa."[10]

Of course, adoptive and reformulated family grandparent relationships will not all be alike. There will be many variables—the age of the children (and the grandparents) when it begins, how close together they live, how frequently they see each other, what access is allowed or encouraged, and what other grandparent figures are in the picture, to name a few. With flexibility as to what experiences to have and what form the relationship takes, these can be lovely, life affirming grandparent experiences on both ends.

INFORMAL "SERENDIPITY"
GRANDPARENT RELATIONSHIPS

But we have not exhausted how people venture into these relationships. Beyond birth, adoption, and new family formulations, there are sometimes more informal connections. In some incidental or accidental connection, two people just "click." This, in turn, may develop into a caring grandparent-like relationship

Stassen Berger tells of a white grandmother in Arizona who welcomed a young Black stranger to dinner. This woman mistakenly texted a Thanksgiving invitation to Jamal Hinton, a Black seventeen-year-old young man. As he didn't recognize the number, he replied, "Who are you?" When she responded, "Your grandmother," he asked for a screenshot. She sent him one. He wrote back, "You not my grandma," with his own selfie attached. But then he added, "Can I still get a plate tho?"

She responded, "Of course you can, that's what grandmas do . . . feed everyone." And so he came to dinner, welcomed by this grandma and her whole family. She invited him back the next year and the next, and he came.[11]

Years ago I had one of those serendipities, a bonding that still warms my heart. It was 1996. I was in Myanmar/Burma as part of my sabbatical, offering classes and sessions on pastoral care and counseling. I had flown into Mandalay, where a professor from a seminary in Pin Oo Lwin would meet me and arrange our transportation for the one-and-a-half-to-two-hour ride to where I would spend the week visiting and teaching. The professor they sent was Lau Nan Ah Sah Mee, who taught pastoral counseling in the seminary I was to visit. I had heard her speak at a conference, but we had not met.

She had secured a driver and car, and so we set on our way, visiting. I was in the front seat with the driver in his ancient taxi, and she was in the back. Almost immediately, we discovered we had much in common. We were both pastors' kids, orphaned of our fathers at an early age, grew up poor (much worse in Burma!), and had strong mothers who did all they could for our education. We had both discovered our love of pastoral counseling, had greatly benefitted from clinical pastoral education, had birthdays in July, and were left-handed!

We spent any spare time that week together, sometimes discussing her work on her in-process dissertation. During one of those conversations, I playfully suggested we should adopt each other. She took to that readily and started calling me Father. I learned that her name translated into English is something like "beautiful third child, woman." When I asked the year of her birth, it was indeed, after the date of our second daughter's birthday and before the birth of our third!

It was very hard to leave after that week! Later, my family, my church, and I were able to provide the modest fee for surgery for an ovarian cyst, surgery she needed but could not afford. Later still, she invited me to come back to Burma to walk her down the aisle at her wedding. Regretfully, I could not.

I have only seen her once since that week at her seminary. She came to the United States for a theological educators' conference and we had her in our home for a couple days. Now, she and her husband serve a Burmese church in Australia and have two young adult children. I have Burmese grandchildren I have never seen. We are in touch at least once a year—the week of those July birthdays. She tells me she has told her children about me and what we did for her. In addition to my own greatly loved family—children, grandchildren, and great-grandchildren—I am so enriched to have a daughter and grandchildren by that serendipity.

As these stories reveal, there are special relationships that can develop unexpectedly out of some connection between people. Call them what you will, I think some of them, at least, are possible grandparent connections.

Still More: Old-Grand-Parents

There is still another possibility to consider: being the "old parent" to any who might need or welcome the attention, friendship, or assistance from older adults who have those gifts to give. For example, when Meri Kay and Trent received their child to adopt, an older friend told them, "This little boy is going to have more grandparents than any child I know—everyone in the church thinks of him as their grandson." That was a promise well kept, as church friends provided not only equipment and supplies, but interest, attention, and encouragement for the child and family through the years.

I have known a number of older adults who support and share the care of children. They undergird the efforts of the children's primary caregivers. Older adults (including some who have no biological or adoptive grandchildren) find a satisfying role as—for lack of better terms—"old parents." Consider a few who have found their way into this adventure.

Phil

Phil had been a faithful member of a church, quiet, introverted, introspective. When his wife died, people wondered how Phil would fill his days. Eventually, he found a way: He volunteered at his church's preschool and its Sunday school and children's programs. He would tell stories, be another chaperone on the playground, rock and comfort unhappy children, and make himself useful in many ways. He became known as the church's grandpa and was much mourned when he died.

Nettie

Nettie offered helpful respite to her young pastor's wife who found herself distracted when trying to hold a squirming one-year-old during worship. Nettie would take the little girl and hold her during worship, letting her explore a large purse filled with interesting and safe objects.

When this child's grandmother became seriously ill, Nettie cared for the child at their farm home while the parents visited the grandmother in the hospital. As the child grew, Nettie found all sorts of interesting things to teach the child, such as how to feed the chickens (and not eat the feed herself), and how to gather eggs without breaking them. Words could not express how much this couple (us!) needed this support and were sustained by it.

Charles and Lorraine

It had become clear that neither of Charles and Lorraine's children would be providing them grandchildren. However, a younger clergy couple, their good friends and colleagues, had two little girls. Charles and Lorraine took a great interest in these girls, sometimes having them over, learning their interests and helping them discover new ones. As these girls aged, Charles and Lorraine contributed to their educational expenses. And as the years went by, there was no doubt they had become family, perhaps surrogate grandparents to these young women whose friendship they treasured so highly.

Walter

When asked about grandchildren, Walter said he had none. However, as he listened to others share their stories, he recalled that his wife and he had provided housing and a home for an international student at the local university for a year or more on at least three occasions. These had led to ongoing relationships, including attending weddings and celebrating births in these (now former) students' lives. Maybe grandparenting was not as remote as he thought.

These are but a few of the possibilities to offer care for busy parents, too often isolated from their own extended families as they raise their children. Herein lies an opportunity, perhaps a calling, for some who might have seen themselves as grandchildless.

Indeed, in today's world, 20 to 25 percent of women of childbearing age are not having any children. There are numbers of people, like Charles and Lorraine, who had looked forward to being biological or adoptive grandparents but who will not.

I have known people who have dwelt on this fact of life. They bemoaned their fate, lamenting what wonderful grandparents they would have been. Others have found somebody else's children and grandchildren to love in many sorts of different ways—and all have been the richer for it.

For all of us who are grandparents in any of the ways I have mentioned—to what are we called out of our love for these children? What is our vocation as grandparents?

FOR INDIVIDUAL OR GROUP REFLECTION

1. How did you become a grandparent? What are your memories of that time? What emotions did you experience? If you had a spouse/partner, how did your experiences and emotions compare?
2. How many, of the various ways mentioned in this chapter, have you "become" a grandparent?
3. What are your impressions and experiences of grandparenthood by adoption? What was your role in the adoption experience?
4. Have you had any "grandparent-like" experiences of connection where you and the person were just drawn to each other? If so, how did it happen?
5. What opportunities or experiences have you had offering grandparent like support to those who could benefit from it?
6. This book encourages us to recognize and follow the calling or vocation that comes from being grandparent. What are you discovering, or perhaps wondering, about what your vocation as grandparent may be?

NOTES

1. Mary Pipher, *Another Country: Navigating the Emotional Terrain of Our Elders* (New York: Riverhead Books, 1999), 287.

2. Lesley Stahl, *Becoming Grandma: The Joys and Science of the New Grandparenting* (New York: Blue Rider Press, 2016), 1

3. Stahl, *Becoming Grandma*, 11–12.

4. Stahl, *Becoming Grandma*, 27–28.

5. Stahl, *Becoming Grandma*, 56

6. Kathleen Stassen Berger, *Grandmothering: Building Strong Ties with Every Generation* (Lanham, MD: Rowman & Littlefield, 2019), 123.

7. "How to Adopt a Child," WikiHow, accessed February 14, 2022, https://www.wikihow.com/Adopt-a-Child.

8. Rebecca Lake, "Average Cost of Adoption in the US," *The Balance*, accessed February 14, 2022, https://www.thebalance.com/average-cost-of-adoption-in-the-u-s-4582452.

9. Stassen Berger, *Grandmothering*, 199–200.

10. Laura Tropp, *Grandparents in a Digital Age: The Third Act* (Lanham, MD: Lexington Books, 2019), 48.

11. Stassen Berger, *Grandmothering*, 41.

Chapter 3

A Pause for Perspective—
How We Got Here

"How very good and pleasant it is when kindred live together in unity!"

—Psalm 133:1

"The role of a grandparent in America in the twenty-first century is ambiguous, peripheral, and negotiated on a family-by-family, individual-by-individual basis."

—Josh Mulvihill[1]

Shortly we will explore all kinds of possible roles we can fill with our grandchildren. Before that, however, we pause to consider what grandparenting used to be like and the several ways it has changed. This may raise some questions about grandparenting we didn't know we had.

While the intergenerational family has been a way of life for many, scholars don't entirely agree as to how much families lived together intergenerationally in the first centuries of settlement in America. Certainly, there were farming families in which the father/grandfather held title to the property as long as he lived. Children and their families worked together under his ownership and direction. Family members who earned their living other ways might live nearby.

Still, intergenerational families were more than an economic arrangement. There might be intergenerational family warmth as well as mutual support and teamwork on large projects. Further, it was a widespread assumption that frail elders would turn to family to be housed and cared for in those fragile final days and years.

GRANDPARENTS AS AUTHORITY FIGURES

In early, preindustrial America, the elderly, including grandparents, were afforded great respect and important roles, for at least two reasons. For one, there were proportionally so few elders. For the other, there was their educational contribution. In preindustrial societies, people were largely illiterate and depended on those who possessed important knowledge and skills to pass them down by demonstration and word of mouth.[2]

But there was also a much shorter life span in those days. Life expectancy expanded some twenty-five to thirty years in the twentieth century alone. In 1900, the life expectancy was forty-six for males and forty-eight for females. For many women, there was probably no—or a very small—distinct "grandmother period" in their lives. The birth of their last child and of their first grandchild might overlap or come very close together. And, on the average, they would not live a great many years beyond the birth of that grandchild.

For many reasons—tradition, scarcity, knowledge/wisdom, economics, and perhaps more—grandparents as the head of the extended family held great power and authority. There was often a religious component to this authority. The elders received, participated in, and handed down a faith and a faith community with beliefs, moral teachings, and religious observances. It was expected that family members would follow their elders' example.

This way of being family has evolved over the years. These changes accelerated in the twentieth century. Scholars Brian Gratton and Carole Haber suggest that the history of American grandparents falls into three phases: authority figures, burdens, and companions.[3]

GRANDPARENTS AS BURDENS

Up to now in this chapter, we have been speaking of the "authority" period of grandparenting. As the Industrial Revolution came and spread, families dispersed to where employment might be available, often far away from the extended family. Housing in industrial cities tended to be smaller, large enough for a nuclear family but not much more. In a rural society, there were responsibilities for everyone, including chores and tasks for the elderly, but not so much in an industrial city. As a result, grandparents' place moved from a traditional position "of authority and esteem to one of obsolescence and dependence." More and more, there developed "interpretations of aging as a disease" and "perception[s] of aging parents and grandparents as a burden to society and to the family."[4]

There were indications in the 1920s and 1930s that the era of obsolescence and being a burden had come for grandparents. For some families, rather than willingly welcoming a frail older relative into a nuclear family home for treatment of illness and/or end of life care, there was reluctance and resistance. Can they not care for themselves?

Josh Mulvihill cites an essay written anonymously for *Harper's* magazine in 1931 in which the author describes elderly parents as disruptive to family life and a cause of family dysfunction.

She writes in part, "[Since grandparents moved in] harmony is gone. Rest has vanished. My husband and I have no longer any time together unless we leave the house. We have no leisure. We have no time for children. . . . We have had to shut our door to hospitality."[5] Out of this, the author of this essay declares that she will want little to do with children and grandchildren in her aging years! Quite probably, she was not speaking just for herself but for many.

A beginning answer to this need for distance from each other arose in the 1930s with the initiation of Social Security. Indeed, by the middle of the twentieth century, older adults were, on the average, in a much better place economically, thanks to Social Security benefits, private pensions, and sometimes, better pay. Of course, this prosperity was spread unevenly and did not touch all grandparents.

When it did, this made it possible for many grandparents to live independently of their children. Steven Ruggles, who has studied residence patterns, notes that in the 1850s, more than 60 percent of old people shared a home with their children. Currently, 15 percent or less do.[6] This was a change in family structure and living relationships that seemed to meet with widespread approval. (However, the proportion of homes with grandparents in residence varies widely from ethnic group to ethnic group.)

GRANDPARENTS AS COMPANIONS

So if grandparents had moved beyond the period of being authority figures and that of being burdens, who or what would they be to their grandchildren? That was a question being studied and pondered in the second half of the twentieth century.

In 1964, family sociologists Bernice L. Neugarten and Karol K. Weinstein published a study, "The Changing American Grandparent," where they reported the discoveries from interviewing seventy pairs of grandparents, all middle class, all living separately from their families.

They found that roughly 70 percent of these grandparents were comfortable in the role of grandparent and 30 percent were not.

As to what significance they found in being grandparents, they spoke of:

- biological continuity,
- emotional fulfillment,
- being a resource to the child, and
- celebrating the grandchild's successes.

Again, nearly 30 percent reported that being a grandparent had little effect on them.

As they asked about grandparenting style, they found a variety of responses. There were:

- the formal relationship (a proper and prescribed role),
- the fun seeker (informality and playfulness), and
- the surrogate parent (actual caretaking of the child).

The researchers also asked about the role of being a reservoir of family wisdom—implying an authoritarian patri-centered relationship, and they found only a tiny response. And there were also just a few very distant from their grandchildren.

Their important study discovered both uncertainty and a wide variety of grandparent responses. However, one thing was certain—it hardly occurred to anyone that the authoritarian grandparent role was still alive![7]

This might bring us to the third part of the history of grandparent relationships—that of companion. Mulvihill points out, however, that with the older roles rejected or left behind, a new role was not clearly defined. This might mean that the grandparent role, if any, was an extra, "a role not essential to the functioning of the family or the growth and development of children." It could feel unclear as to what was welcome or allowed in the child's family. While there might be great affection and enjoyment in grandparent-grandchild experiences, there was uncertainty as well.

Mulvihill concludes, "Grandparents became companions to their grandchildren as independence meant they had no authoritative position or important economic role in the family."[8]

And so, as we grandparents love, enjoy, and bring gifts to our grandchildren, there might be an important question to ponder: Is anything missing? Is there anything not being addressed in my grandchild's growth, becoming, developing, discovering, achieving? If something is missing, is it something I could contribute in some way? If I do so, is it okay? Am I permitted? Should I ask permission? If my grandchildren's parents divorce, am I still permitted contact and influence? Am I even allowed contact? Is my presence and contribution needed even more?

GRANDPARENTING IN THE TWENTY-FIRST CENTURY

Today, grandparents and their families are heirs of the traditions we have described, but we live in even more changed and changing circumstances. For example, Kathleen Stassen Berger, speaking specifically for her present cohort of grandmothers, describes how grandmothers have changed, even while the culture has not. She notes:

1. We have had jobs; many grandmothers still do, . . . In the 1970s, millions of mothers joined the work force.
2. We are educated. My cohort has far more high school graduates and college degrees (including JDs, MDs, and PhDs) than our foremothers.
3. We live longer.
4. We live healthier.
5. We are mentally more alert.
6. We had fewer babies. Our children have even fewer (and have them later), often only one.[9]

These changes impact all of us grandparents. In the twenty-first century, life expectancy has continued to increase (with a couple of blips, most recently from the COVID pandemic). And so now, persons can expect to spend almost half of their lives as grandparents. There is a 50 percent chance, at least, of being great-grandparent. Three-quarters of all Americans, 94 percent of those with children, are or will be grandparents.

However, the number of grandchildren per grandparent is much reduced. Stassen Berger notes that her grandmother had twenty-two grandchildren; her mother, seventeen; and she, three—and still, that is a bit above the trend. She speaks of a new crisis—"the grandmother glut and birth dearth." The world now has more adults over the age of fifty than children under fifteen. Fertility is below replacement rate of the population in more than eighty countries.

Worldwide, the average woman had 5 children in 1950; she has 2.5 now. In the United States, the fertility rate was 3.3 births per woman in 1950; it was 1.9 in 2015.[10] Clearly, grandparenting will be longer, with opportunities along the life stages of children and grandparents. However, it will be with a much smaller group of grandchildren, who, in all likelihood, are shared with other grandparents, great-grandparents, aunts and uncles, and great-aunts and great-uncles.

The question remains: What roles should responsible grandparents play? So far in this chapter we have provided *description* of the ways grandparenthood has changed. What about *prescription*?

Mulvihill summarizes how, in his view, grandparents in America feel about their role:

- Powerless—as compared with earlier grandparents who knew so much their grandchildren didn't,
- Role-less—retired with "nothing to do and no one to do anything for,"
- Disconnected—with one's own parents dead and one's children not needing them,
- Superannuated—not experiencing benefits of a long, healthy life because of isolation and disconnection,
- Disoriented—by confusion about what to do about all this, and
- Replaced—by "impersonal institutions, services, and personnel" that now fill in the vacuum that grandparents have left.[11]

How do you respond to that list of descriptors for us grandparents? Does it feel a bit overstated? Or does it touch some concerns that grandparents may feel vaguely but find hard to raise and address?

Ruth K. Westheimer and Stephen Kaplan further explore this confused situation. They write, "Of all the roles in the nuclear and extended family, none is as loosely defined as that of the grandparents." They, too, note the grandparental role has often been seen as "vague, ambiguous, role less, or even empty." They conclude that "many grandparents, especially first-timers, are often left unsure of what is expected of them and how best to fill their role."[12]

At very least, for all of us who delight in our grandchildren, these scholars raise important questions for us. It comes down to this: What does my grandchild and the child's family need from me? What do we have to offer? For all our delight in each other, what more beckons? Where does my vocation as a Christian, and specifically a Christian grandparent, come into this? These are the topics we will consider in the next chapters

FOR PERSONAL AND GROUP REFLECTION

1. What, if any, memories does this chapter raise for you? Aha moments? Questions?
2. How many of the themes of authority figure, burden, and companion did you witness in your grandparents? In your parents? In your role as grandparent?
3. If you had contact with your grandparents, what impressions did you have? How did they relate to you? What roles did they play with you?
4. From any of those grandparent memories, what would you like to replicate with your grandchildren? What would you like to avoid? Replace?

5. Our constant theme in this book is grandparenting as a vocation for the afternoon and evening of life. What clues did you detect about your vocation of grandparenthood in this chapter?

NOTES

1. Josh Mulvihill, *Biblical Grandparenting: Exploring God's Design for Disciple-Making and Passing Faith to Future Generations* (Minneapolis: Bethany House, 2018), 121.

2. Brian Gratton and Carole Haber, "Three Phases in the History of American Grandparents: Authority, Burden, Companion," *Generations* 20, no.1 (1996): 13, as cited in Mulvihill, *Biblical Grandparenting*, 91.

3. Gratton and Haber, "Three Phases in the History of American Grandparents."

4. "Grandparenthood," Encyclopedia.com, accessed September 1, 2021, https://www.encyclopedia.com/social-sciences-and-law/sociology-and-social-reform/sociology-general-terms-and-concepts/grandparent.

5. "Old Age Intestate," *Harper's* 162 (May 1931) 712–713, as reported in Mulvihill, *Biblical Grandparenting*, 92–93.

6. Cited in Mulvihill, *Biblical Grandparenting*, 94.

7. Bernice L. Neugarten and Karol K. Weinstein, "The Changing American Grandparent," *Journal of Marriage and Family* 16, no. 2 (May 1964): 199–204.

8. Mulvihill, *Biblical Grandparenting*, 95.

9. Kathleen Stassen Berger, *Grandmothering: Building Strong Ties with Every Generation* (Lanham: Rowman & Littlefield, 2017), 8–9.

10. Stassen Berger, *Grandmothering*, 9, 12, 90.

11. Mulvihill, *Biblical Grandparenting*, 130, He in turn cites Arthur Kornhaber and Kenneth L. Woodward, *Grandparents/Grandchildren: The Vital Connection* (New York: Routledge, 2019).

12. Ruth K. Westheimer and Steven Kaplan, *Grandparenthood* (New York: Routledge, 1998), 50.

Chapter 4

Discerning My Unique Grandparent Role(s)

"Now there are varieties of gifts, but the same Spirit; and there are varieties of services, but the same Lord."

—1 Corinthians 12:4–5

"A new type of grandparenting is arising, serving both familiar roles and new ones as well."

—Laura Tropp[1]

What is my calling with these grandchildren and their families, in these changing times and journeys that have brought us together? How can I contribute to these children's joy, well-being, and becoming? To their faith and spiritual journey?

Our roles may vary. Different children may need different things from us. Or families will.

In this chapter we will explore a wide variety of possibilities. Some will be mentioned only briefly, as other chapters will describe them in more detail. Here is a cornucopia of possible grandparent roles that may be possible for you or needed from you.

ANCESTOR, HISTORIAN, GRIOT

Obviously, we are among our grandchildren's ancestors. We have experiences and recollections of years before they were born and memories of decades even before that—our parents and grandparents. All of this can be an important gift in helping children know who they are and what heritage they continue.

This is even more important than may appear at first glance. Bruce Feiler recalls a time when his extended family was together and they found themselves in a time of tension, both within and between different parts of the family. They feared they were falling apart. He recalls, "I began to wonder: . . . what is the secret sauce that holds a family together? What are the ingredients that make some families effective, resilient, happy?"[2]

As he searched for answers to those questions, one insight was that children who know a lot about their families do better when they face challenges. Feiler discovered this as he learned about the research of two psychologists from Emory University. Marshall Duke and Robyn Fivush created a set of twenty questions about family, titled "Do You Know?" This included such questions as: "Do you know where your grandparents grew up? . . . where your mom and dad went to high school? . . . how your parents met? . . . something terrible that happened in your family? . . . the story of your birth?"

They discovered that as children learned more about their family's history, their sense of control over their lives became stronger.[3]

Duke points out that it is important for a child's well-being to sense they are part of a larger family. Their family story may have one of three themes. The first is the "ascending family narrative"—how their family started with very little and achieved. The second is the "descending family narrative"— how their family had much but lost all or most of it. The most healthful is the third, the "oscillating family narrative"—we have had our ups and downs, but we stuck together and overcame the difficulties.

Out of knowing such family stories, children develop what these researchers call a "strong intergenerational self," which is to say "they know the belong to something bigger than themselves."[4] This in turn may contribute to a child's "higher levels of self-esteem, . . . a belief in one's capacity to control what happens to him or her, better family functioning, lower levels of anxiety, fewer behavioral problems and better chances for good outcome if a child faced educational or emotional/behavioral difficulties."[5]

So clearly, we have a gift to offer as ancestor, family historian, and family griot. (A griot is an African storyteller whose stories may span the generations and centuries.) This set of twenty questions is provided in appendix A for your use and conversation in your family.

There are also many other ways to perform this role of historian. For example, twice I have offered something written to members of my family. When my mother died, my sister and I put together our memories of our parents and some genealogical information the family might not have otherwise accessed and gave it to all members of our family. We called it *Roots and Wings—One Family's Story*. Later, aware that I grew up in a different world than my grandchildren—small town, poor, no car, no indoor plumbing, and so on—I wrote a book of true stories of my childhood for my grandchildren. I adapted the title of a well-known TV show for its title, *Little House in a Little Town on the Prairie.*

For those who are not writers, there are many other ways to pass along this history. Perhaps photograph albums, or scrapbooks can tell some of the story, stir questions, and inspire storytelling. Younger grandparents might do this electronically. Pictures of ancestors on the walls, or perhaps of the weddings of parents and grandparents, are reminders. One person recalls how exciting it was that there was a trunk of items, old clothes and all, from the Civil War days that she could explore and try on. And, of course, there's good old-fashioned storytelling out loud.

Trips can offer historical perspective. I remember a vacation where we went to my grandparents' homestead. My father took me to what was then a large mound of dirt and told me that it had been the sod house where they lived—and where he had been born, in fact! A trip to a graveyard where ancestors are buried can bring part of the family story together.

One of our roles is to contribute to our grandchildren's self-awareness, family membership, and personal strength is by telling stories. In so doing we invite discovery of "this is who we were, and this is who we are."

TEACHER, MENTOR, STUDENT

In this new and different world, we grandparents are wise to combine learning and teaching roles with our grandchildren. A specific memory comes to mind as I say this. It was June 1998. My family had come for the farewell celebration as I retired from parish ministry.

At the end of the banquet, I was given some gifts. As my church friends knew I liked to write, one of the gifts was a new laptop computer that used Windows software. I had previously used a computer with the old DOS system. As I said my closing thank you, I was quietly wondering if I would ever learn how to use the new system. Five minutes later, as I was greeting friends and telling them goodbye, I looked down and saw that my seven-year-old granddaughter was playing solitaire on my new computer! It inspired a limerick—

> I'm learned, I'm told, wise and smart.
> I know tomes and some poems each by heart.
> So I'm humbled to see
> Tis a child and not me—
> Who can get this computer to start!

Clearly, this grandchild, then and in the years after, had much she could teach me—how to navigate the internet, how to set up a Facebook page, and so much more. But she would have to slow down and learn to be as patient with Grandpa as he tried to be patient with her!

These days, my pair of two-year-old great-grandsons love to play with my phone. One immediately finds the camera and takes pictures; the other will at least find the calculator and play with numbers on it. I can only imagine what they will have to teach Great-Grandpa by the time they are five! They have been born into and will grow into a technological culture that I often struggle to navigate.

But beyond that, Kerry Byrne guides us, "ask your grandchild this: What do you know how to do that you can teach me?"

This is a question of respect to a grandchild of any age. Byrne further notes, "For little ones this might be a song." Older children may have a range of topics where their studies and interests are more recent and informed than those of their grandparents. She concludes, "Whatever it is, asking them to teach you will let them know how much you value their knowledge."[6] Wise is the grandparent who respects the grandchild and shows it by learning from them!

But we are also teachers. As mentioned in chapter 2, in earlier times grandparents were among the elders revered for all the knowledge, wisdom, and skills they possessed to teach the next—mostly illiterate—generation. Our grandchildren have many channels of information and their tech knowledge is certainly superior to ours, but still, there is important teaching we can offer the next generations. Indeed, we need to remember that we bear wisdom, perspective, and experience in living out of the important things we have to teach.

And so our opportunity is also to offer ourselves as mentors and teachers with them as well. The term *mentor* refers to a way of being and of teaching. The emphasis is on the person, not the subject. Our goal is not so much instant mastery of whatever topic, but rather the relationship, the affirmation, the encouragement, the person's development. Further, quite possibly, there is subtle teaching by example. My grandparent message as mentor is, "I love being with you. You are so special to me. Whatever we do or discover will be extra special because we are doing it together. Together, we will discover more and be more than either of us could by ourselves."

This atmosphere can occasion all sorts of teaching where neither of us knows that is what is happening. Grandparent and grandchild are simply enjoying an activity together. This may be cooking, baking, sewing, knitting, crocheting, gardening, building, hunting, fishing, reading, writing, and so much more. One grandchild told me he learned to love baseball from listening to games of the local professional team on the radio with his grandmother and discussing them. I taught a little basketball and baseball to my grandchildren, mostly just playing with them.

Mary Ann was such a teacher of her sewing and quilting skills. When one of our granddaughters expressed an interest, Mary Ann arranged for her to come to our home for a time. The first week, she sent our granddaughter and the daughter of friends to a children's sewing class offered in our community. The next week, each of them selected a project and picked out fabrics. Then she guided them, step by step, to its successful completion.

Out of this grew a "quilt camp" where grandma, a daughter, and two granddaughters from different families would gather for a week of sewing on their various quilting projects together. Other family members who were not quilters were not invited! When quilt camp met at our house, I was told the ground rules: I could take our granddaughters swimming if they wanted a break and asked me to take them. But I could not put my head in the work room and ask, "Anyone want to go swimming with me?" No outside interruptions allowed!

Such teaching may also address significant learning needs. A boy who was dyslexic had failed first grade and was embarrassed and discouraged. His grandmother patiently worked with him so that he could gain the skills needed to proceed with his age group—to his profound gratitude. Or such teaching might involve helping a grandchild's unique gifts and skills progress even further.

WIZARD, STORYTELLER

Arthur Kornhaber notes that "there is a deep human need for fantasy throughout life." This is true of all ages but perhaps young children, most of all, "especially benefit from imaginative play." Small children may have an imaginary friend or pet that is very real to them. And so, he invites, "Your role as a wizard for your grandchild is one of the most enjoyable freewheeling, and free-spirited roles you will ever play."[7]

Nan recalls walks with her grandpa where their imaginations would soar. They saw a beautiful eagle one day and made up a story about what it would be like to be an eagle. Another day, it was a woodchuck they discovered, and they created a fantasy about how this little animal managed his days and his life. Her grandpa later took her to see an actual woodchuck's nest so they could expand on their earlier fantasies.

Another grandpa would sit in his car with his young grandson. He would point to the horn and it would go off or to the window and the windshield wipers would start—to his grandson's delight. He thought his grandpa was a magician, not noticing that his grandpa's other hand was manipulating the controls.[8]

One of my granddaughters in particular loved fantasy and drew me into imaginary worlds with her. Once, when I was visiting them in winter, she wanted the two of us to put on our outside clothes, for we were going on a journey. She took me into their backyard area where there was a small wooded section, probably not larger than forty by forty feet. Still, for more than an hour she led me on a journey, going through those small woods at every possible angle, hiding out from danger, getting hungry and capturing and preparing food, setting up camp for the "night," rising early and moving on. I was getting colder and colder, but she didn't seem to notice the cold until finally our journey was completed and we went inside. My fantasy gift that day was to see what she saw and enter her world.

A few years later, she was a guest in our home. I was to care for her during the day while her mother and grandmother took part in a weeklong quilting class. I had in mind a number of places we could go, things we could see, events we could attend. But she wanted none of that. She wanted us to stay home, perhaps in our screened-in back porch or wandering around our backyard. And we would make up stories. Sometimes I listened to her stories and sometimes she wanted to hear mine. I hadn't invented children's stories since her mother was a child. Back then I had created a "Grumpy Bear" who got himself into and out of all sorts of trouble, problems, and difficulties. With a little nudging, Grumpy Bear came back to life and took us through a few shenanigans. Sometimes we would pass the story back and forth, taking turns making it up.

By the end of the week, I was experiencing "imagination exhaustion." Still, I treasure having been invited into that fantasy world with a grandchild and enjoyed every stimulating moment!

For grandparents who may not feel talented in wizardry, it can be learned, in my experience. Be open and accepting of your grandchild's imagination. Follow their lead, be inquisitive, be accepting, and you may be invited to a world you have never seen before!

The stories of your own childhood may also have an otherworldly, fantasy quality for your grandchildren. You may be wizard simply by telling about growing up in another time and place!

Also, there are wonderful books for children that tell the stories of such adventures. These can be read, enjoyed, and discussed together.

PLAYMATE, JOKESTER, PRANKSTER

The next chapter is devoted to this topic, so for now I will just mention this part of our possible grandparent roles. When grandchildren arrive, one of the delights is the rediscovery and reexperiencing of childhood. From birth on, adults will make funny faces and strange sounds if it seems to please the baby. The delights of peek-a-boo and hide-and-seek are rediscovered. Games are brought out of storage or repurchased. For many grandparents, this is just a tug, a lure to return to play and laughter. This can be a source of great enjoyment for both grandparent and grandchild. Grandchildren can bring out our inner child and enrich our world.

I remember a playful time when our grandson, then about ten or so, was visiting. My wife frequently said, "Oh honestly, Dick," when expressing mild disapproval or frustration. She wasn't aware how often she said it, though the rest of the family was. One day, my grandson and I did an experiment: I would see how many times I could get her to say it in a day, and he would count and keep track. I think I got her up to about a dozen. I assure you it was done in a spirit of play and affection, no disrespect intended.

Sadly, when she became aware of how often she was saying these words and the family's jokes about it, she quit saying them.

Friendly jokes, playful teasing, games, competitions, and more—these are treasured activities made possible and encouraged by delighted grandparents.

RELIGIOUS/SPIRITUAL PRESENCE, MODEL, OR GUIDE

This aspect of grandparenting is explored in much more detail in chapter 10. For now, I would like to note its possible significance as a role. With the various marriages and journeys of children and grandchildren, they may be in a similar place or a far different one than you with regard to religious heritage and conviction (and the political beliefs that sometimes go with it).

While respecting these differences, a grandparent can be witness and example of the heritage from which they came and the faith they now hold. This may be an option to which grandchildren may want to return some day.

I recall a conversation I had with my geriatric nurse practitioner, Maira, who is a compassionate and skillful care provider. I asked her how she got into geriatrics, and after a moment of reflection she responded, "My grandma and I were very close." I asked her to tell me more, and this, in part, is what she said: "On Saturdays she would take me to church. Grandma was very active at our local church. She was responsible for fundraisings and gathering donations for the poor. She helped so many people. Grandma touched my life in so many ways, but her generosity and kindness helped shape my personal and professional goals in life today."[9]

We grandparents are the roots of the family in many ways. By practicing what we believe with integrity, we may be our family's spiritual and religious roots.

COUNTERCULTURAL HERO

In myth and story, a hero is someone with courage and strength who uses these gifts creatively to serve some great end. Arthur Kornhaber points out that children need heroes. Their parents may fill this role in some ways, "but grandparents, because they are a bit more removed and have a broader range of experience, can be heroes with an added dimension, one that is a bit more connected to the mythic." He adds, "These days a grandparent's heroic role is needed more than ever because public heroes are in short supply."[10]

Grandparents lived in an earlier time and a different place. They survived, maybe even prospered, and they helped family members in their growing, learning, and achieving. In all this, grandparents have attained some of the stuff of being heroes.

Grandparents may also have had illnesses, hospitalizations, or surgery— and they came through it. They may have had to learn to walk again with a cane or a walker. Particularly if they do this with a minimum of complaint and a sense of the joy of living, they are performing heroically.

This is in a time when there is ageism—widespread prejudice and disdain for the elderly in our culture. So grandparents have the opportunity to model and teach about respect and admiration for old people. This is particularly true for old people who know how to face adversity, live well, and care about others.

NURTURER, COMFORTER, ADVOCATE, CHEERLEADER

Grandparents also have a calling basically to be there when needed. From infancy on, whenever a helping hand or a strong shoulder is needed, grandparents might be the first on call. When children are asked what grandparents do, they most frequently answer, "They worry about us." Exactly. Constructive worry offers concrete help when possible.

If family tensions, breakup, or divorce happens, grandparents can be the nurturers to upset children, assuring them of continuing care and stability. When children are sick or injured, a grandparent may be there. A grandparent's quiet presence, perhaps reading stories or making a comforting soup, may help pass the time of the too-slow healing and recovery.

Another aspect of this role is that while there unfortunately may be "favorite" children in a family, there should never be a "favorite" grandchild. Rather, it is the grandparent's calling to make *each* grandchild the favorite one. This may mean being the encourager for the one who is struggling or dealing with some handicap, the silent companion to the quiet or shy one, the appreciator of the grandchild whose interests may not be as public or flashy as a sibling's.

Always, there is opportunity to affirm and build up each grandchild. Richard Eyre speaks of a "simple principle" that he is discovering and applying even more diligently to his grandchildren than he did to his children: "It is this: *Kids thrive, flourish and blossom in the light of thoughtful, specific, sincere compliments, particularly from their grandfathers.*" He points out that there is a certain amount of insecurity in most people's childhoods. As children compare themselves to schoolmates and celebrities in media and the public eye, they may feel quite inadequate. "In this reality," Eyre says, "sometimes a well-placed compliment, coming from a grandpa, can have a powerful and lasting positive influence."[11] Eyre is writing specifically for grandfathers. I surmise he may also have offered this observation because such compliments are less often coming from us than from their grandmothers.

SAFETY NET

Still another angle on this role is to see ourselves as—and make the family aware that we are—a "safety net" for our grandchildren. As Ruth Westheimer and Stephen Kaplan note, with all the threats in our world, "what better role to fill than that of an island of stability in a sea of change?" Further, they write, "In a world of runaway change, grandparents have a vital role to play in providing security and consistency . . . [which means] . . . that whatever changes take place in our life, your grandchildren always know they can depend on you."[12] Furthermore, they note, teaching grandchildren that they can depend on you is also teaching them that they can depend on themselves.

This role may be claimed in times of crisis, but it becomes an available resource if built up by many smaller experiences. These may include good listening, providing a sympathetic ear a shoulder to cry on. Out of many caring interventions, a child or youth may know where to turn when all else has failed.

CONFIDANT

In families at their best, children and young people talk freely and openly. However, there are times when the young may want to confide in some other adult than their parents. This could be a teacher, coach, or counselor. At times it may be a grandparent.[13]

The key to trust, of course, is the ability to keep a secret. Of course, grandparents should not fail to inform parents of the child is doing something illegal, is in danger, or may be suicidal. There is widespread wisdom that when one is a threat to oneself or others, confidentiality should be suspended, and certainly, this applies here.

But on many matters—perhaps embarrassing, delicate, uncertain, possibly a hope or aspiration, or a confusion—confidentiality is needed. A caring adult who will listen, respond when asked, and keep quiet about the matter can be a treasured resource indeed.

ECOLOGIST

This important role will be explored in more detail in chapter 9. Here, it is worth noting simply that one of the productive ways for grandparents to worry is about this planet on which their grandchildren will live. All the ways a grandparent can practice protecting the environment—and all the ways they can teach and do these practices with their grandchildren—are essential roles to play. Citizen advocacy and lobbying for wise environmental legislation, practices, and controls beckons the caring grandparent.

FITNESS AND HEALTH ADVOCATE

Arthur Kornhaber, a grandfather who is also a physician, identifies a role he points out is desperately needed—as a fitness and health advocate. He mentions that 71 percent of 9 million US children fail to meet fitness standards for average healthy youngsters. Childhood obesity and youthful use of tobacco, alcohol, and other drugs are all reasons for deep concern. And so he announces, "I'm going to put you in charge of your grandchildren's health and fitness."[14] Wise counsel, guidance, and modeling as regards nutrition, exercise, and moderation may be important grandparent perspectives for a family.

Kornhaber also urges candor about sexuality, for, as he notes, sexually transmitted infections and young pregnancies are public health issues. (A recent AARP survey of grandparents revealed that these topics are among the least likely for grandparents to discuss with grandchildren.)[15] So, whatever our capability and readiness, Kornhaber sounds the alarm. Health advocate is a much-needed role for grandparents who love their grandchildren and want them to be healthy, strong, and effective.

DEVELOPMENTALIST

One more thought that is simple but sometimes hard: An effective grandparent is sensitive and responsive to the growth, change, development, and aging of our grandchildren. Of course, this is obvious. However, when we have adored the infant and loved the toddler, it may be hard to let go. There will be a time to do so, to engage the school-aged child and later the adolescent and young adult.

Richard Eyre approaches this aspect in a playful way. He starts with the idea of "championing" our grandkids. A champion is one who "elevates others as their advocate, encourager, supporter, defender, protector, and opportunity maker." The way this is done, he points out, will change over the years.

For children under age eight, the grandparent-champion is a "Ringmaster," offering them a good time, going places, seeing new things, and having fun experiences: "Enjoy them and let them enjoy you! Be their ringmasters in the circus of their young lives."

For grandkids aged eight through sixteen, the grandparent-champion should "Be a Buddy"—a very special kind of buddy, "one who knows them . . . loves them unconditionally . . . has always believed in them . . . who is always there for them . . . whom they can trust and confide in . . . whom they can tell anything and everything." This may involve a lot of growing for the grandparent, including trying to keep current with them in whatever electronic communications they are using. It involves trying "to evolve with them."

For grandkids older than eighteen, the grandparent-champion should "Be a Consultant." While many still treat them as kids, they need someone who will relate to them as adults. They need a person who is interested in and who respects their opinions. By carefully building an atmosphere of trust, a grandparent may earn the right to be the young adult's "consultant." This is "not a manager or someone who tells you what to do or pushes you around," but rather "someone with . . . experience who can help you with your goals and help you . . . become what you want to be."[16]

Whether we frame this as Eyre did or in our own way, the concept is wise. We treasured our grandchildren's birth, infancy and early years. But mature love grows, changes, responds, and is there at each point along life's journey.

AND SO—

This chapter uses the concept of "roles" as a way to explore aspects of our calling, our vocation as grandparents. As we welcome and grow with our grandchildren, some roles are instinctive. Some emerge out of the child's or the family's needs. And some may be possibilities for grandparents and grandchildren to explore together.

In preparing this chapter, I made my own list of possible roles, talked with many grandparents, and read several other authors' lists. Each source person quickly said that any collection of possibilities is only a beginning, pointing to more ideas to explore.

What do you think? Where does this list of possible roles lead you? What else beckons?

FOR PERSONAL OR GROUP REFLECTION

1. What are your roles with your grandchildren? How did they come about?
2. Which of your roles with your grandchildren are most rewarding? What makes them so? What adventures did you have?
3. What, if any, roles have you left behind? What new possibilities come to mind as your grandchildren grow older?
4. What was missing from the list of possible roles in this chapter? What roles do you have that were not mentioned?
5. What invitations did you hear in this chapter?

NOTES

1. Laura Tropp, *Grandparents in a Digital Age: The Third Act* (Lanham, MD: Lexington Books, 2019), 23.

2. Bruce Feiler, "The Stories That Bind Us," *New York Times*, March 17, 2013, accessed September 10, 2021, https://www.nytimes.com/2013/03/17/fashion/the -family-stories-that-bind-us-this-life.html.

3. Feiler, "The Stories That Bind Us."

4. Feiler, "The Stories That Bind Us."

5. Marshall P. Duke, "The Stories That Bind Us: What Are the Twenty Questions?" *Huffington Post*, March 23, 2013, accessed September 10, 2021, https://www.huffpost .com/entry/the-stories-that-bind-us-_b_2918975.

6. Kerry Byrne, e-mail to the author.

7. Arthur Kornhaber, *The Grandparent Guide: The Definitive Guide to Coping with the Challenges of Modern Grandparenting* (Chicago: Contemporary Books, 2002), 61,63.

8. Kornhaber, *The Grandparent Guide*, 62, 64.

9. Quote used with permission; name withheld for confidentiality.

10. Kornhaber, *The Grandparent Guide*, 17.

11. Richard Eyre, *Being a Proactive Grandfather: How to Make a Difference* (New York: Familius, 2017), 18–19.

12. Ruth Westheimer and Stephen Kaplan, *Grandparenthood* (New York: Routledge, 1998), 72.

13. Westheimer and Kaplan, *Grandparenthood*, 69.

14. Arthur Kornhaber with Sondra Forsyth, *Grandparent Power! How to Strengthen the Vital Connection among Grandparents, Parents, and Children* (New York: Crown, 1994), 91.

15. AARP, "2018 Grandparents Today National Survey," accessed September 17, 2021, https://www.aarp.org/content/dam/aarp/research/surveys_statistics/life-leisure/2019/aarp-grandparenting-study.doi.10.26419-2Fres.00289.001.pdf.

16. Eyer, *Being a Proactive Grandfather*, 16–18. (A few quotes, some summary and paraphrase.)

Chapter 5

Called to Celebration, Laughter, and Play with My Grandchildren

"A merry heart doeth good like a medicine; but a broken spirit drieth up the bones."

—Proverbs 17:22 (KJV)

"The Ojibwa people call old people 'wisdom keepers.' They are treasures. They are also the funniest people in the community. Elders have the freedom to tease anybody."

—Louise Erdrich[1]

"We get the joys of parenting without the midnight stifles and the daytime coughs, without the need for discipline and the demand for obedience. We are the recess, the play period, the respite from the demands made as they learn to live in a confusing world—and so our grandchildren look to us for good times and laughter. Is it any wonder that we think grandchildren are so much fun?"

—Lois Wyse[2]

Lois Wyse may overstate it a bit. Our relationships with our grandchildren will have many dimensions, and sometimes parental concerns may be part of them. Still, she is surely right that laughter, delight, and play are at the very heart of who we are to our grandchildren and who they are to us.

Laughter in our life is good for us! This commonsense statement has now been clinically proven. For example, Georgia Witkin summarizes much of this research that "just 100 laughs a day" (not as hard to accomplish as you might think) will have these benefits:

- Provide an aerobic workout as great as ten minutes on a rowing machine;
- Increase endorphins, which reduce pain and increase a sense of well-being;
- Raise body temperature a bit and give a warm glow;
- Increase pulse rate and blood pressure and in turn sharpen thinking;
- Enhance respiration;
- Relax tension;
- Improve the functioning of the immune system;
- Lower the stress hormone;
- (If belly laughing) strengthen abdominal muscles; and
- Burn calories (amount unknown).[3]

Smiling is good for us also, she notes: "People who smile, even when they don't feel especially happy, can actually change their brain chemistry to mimic happiness. . . . [Further], sadness is blocked, and we feel happy! [And further still], . . . voluntarily producing smiles moves . . . brain activity in the direction of spontaneous happiness."[4] And that is just the interior part. Smiles also have a relationship-building and drawing-close impact on those who receive the smiles.

Witkin points to the physical and psychological good that humor, laughter, and smiling provide us. I believe humor is also a spiritual practice that enhances one's life of faith, of living, loving, and serving God, God's people, and the world.[5] Humor can be a way of gaining perspective, renewing energy, and addressing depression or despair. Humor and laughter can heal and energize. Laughter is good for us, it is good for our grandchildren, and it is just waiting for us.

Babies laugh before they speak! This often happens by three months, but the first words will not come till months later. Laughter is one of the first ways infants engage the world. This fascinated baby scientist Caspar Addyman. As part of their research on this subject, he and his associates sent a set of questions to respondents around the world. The queries included: When did their babies first laugh? What situations do they find the funniest? What toys and games made them laugh the most? They received responses from nearly fifteen hundred mothers and fathers in sixty-two countries around the globe—including the Philippines, Zambia, Uruguay, and Australia.

What was the baby's favorite laugh stimulant, regardless of culture? Peek-a-boo! So, what really makes babies laugh? Addyman says his one-word answer is "people." His two-word answer is "adult attention" or "human connection."

The importance of the human company element in laughter continues into early childhood. Addyman also studied how children aged between two and a half and four years old reacted to a funny cartoon when they watched it alone, with one other child, and in a group. Amazingly, children laughed eight times as much when they watched the cartoon with at least one other child than when they watched it by themselves.[6]

So there we have it: From infancy on, we love to laugh. Other human company either makes us laugh—or, at least, we laugh more when in the company of others. We grandparents delight in those humans who are our grandchildren, and they in us. This opens one of the easiest and enjoyable ways of fulfilling our grandparent vocation: to create and enter those times that stir or enhance our fun and laughter together.

LOVE OF STORY

One of the ways we enjoy each other is with our love of story. I have already mentioned how one of my granddaughters and I would go on make-believe adventures outside or sit on our back porch and make up stories together—one telling for a while, then the other picking up and adding some details, back and forth. Now in her twenties, she is a computer scientist. When we see each other, if we happen to start reminiscing, those magical times come to our minds once more.

Alan says that one of his favorite things to do with his two grandchildren is to take them to a bookstore and tell them how many books each of them can have. He then watches them wander and explore, trying to decide which books hold the greatest promise for their next reading adventure.

Kathleen and her two granddaughters—Olivia, age ten, and Abigail, age eleven—have formed a Harry Potter book club. They have been meeting for a year and a half. The granddaughters have gifted her with a HP (Harry Potter) scarf, which she wears to the meetings. She describes how this club functions: "We first read the book and then watch the movie. Each time we meet, we have a discussion of the part of the book we are reading. There is all sorts of Harry Potter stuff on the table. I have had questions my granddaughters have given me to consider, and I have had assignments given to me. So far, we have read four of the seven books and are taking a break. My granddaughter Abigail will choose a book for us to explore next."

There is joy in exploring a grandchild's imaginary world, whether that of authors they love or of their and our own creation.

GATHERINGS

Building and experiencing community within the extended family can bring great enjoyment. I have mentioned the quilt camp my wife held with a daughter and two granddaughters for a number of years.

Jeanie recalls,

I used to hold "cousin camp" every August with my three oldest grandchildren, all girls, born within five years of each other. They would stay overnight with me a couple nights. We would do all kinds of projects, perhaps some sewing or crafts. For sure we'd do some baking. We'd watch movies and have a "spa day" with makeup, fingernail polish, the works. They would make me up for the day as well. This year, my oldest granddaughter, now twenty-one and a university senior, hosted cousin camp in her college apartment. They told me, "We will invite you to come." "Oh no, I will just take you all out to breakfast," I told them. That worked out beautifully. I was glad they wanted to carry out that tradition. I want them to know each other, feel part of a family.

Kathy loves that she, her children, and her grandchildren spend a week together each summer on one of the lakes in northern Wisconsin. How do they spend the week?

Eating together, fishing together, playing in the water, playing board games—Phase 10, Rummy Cube, dominoes, Catan [a new board game they love]. When I don't get it how to play, they are very patient with me.

Before we go up north, we have a family meeting. Each family brings something. They find the housing. I pay the rent for the week. I don't have to share in the work in any shape or fashion. We have wonderful conversations, much joking, teasing, play.

We do a lot of fishing—mostly catch and release. There are two "traveling trophies," one for biggest fish and one for perseverance. On Friday night we go out to a very nice restaurant. Whoever had the trophy last year presents it to the new winner. Of course, there has to be pictures. We all look forward to family vacation every year.

Their gathering includes a granddaughter who is on the autism spectrum, doing well as adult but with needs for privacy and some silence. The family includes her and makes these provisions for her.

INTENDED OR UNINTENDED CHILDREN'S HUMOR

As our grandchildren grow, they explore and grow into this language we speak. Sometimes what they discover amuses them, and sometimes they happen on a unique expression that entertains us. Either way, language does what it should do—it builds and strengthens bonds between us.

I remember when one of our daughters learned her first riddle: "Where does an elephant put his socks? In his trunk." She would tell it, and an adult would smile or chuckle. So she would tell it to the same person again the next time she saw them, not realizing she'd have to find new material. Such are the joys and the frustrations of language.

The fun goes on. Alan's nine-year-old granddaughter Lilly loves riddles also, but she leaves the old ones behind and goes on to new ones. A few of her favorites:

- What's black and white and red [read] all over? The newspaper.
- Why do bees have sticky hair? Because they comb it with honeycombs.
- Why did the chicken cross the road? Why are you asking me? I don't speak chicken. (This is one of her originals.)

Further, the various meanings of the same simple words can lead to grace notes in misunderstandings. For example, six-year-old Samuel was sitting beside his grandma at services in the temple, when he heard the rabbi recite, "The Lord our God, the Lord is one." Samuel whispered, "Grandma, when will he be two?"[7]

Ron M. loves and enjoys his grandchildren's speech. For example, when four-year-old David was asked how Parents Day Out was, he responded, "It was good. I made up some new friends." Another example: the other day they were playing baseball, and seven-year-old Marie was having a hard time hitting. Her explanation: "I hit like a ballerina, that's why I am spinning all the way around."

I remember another child's (to me, humorous) prank. At age three, one of our granddaughters was impish and lively, some would say a "pill." Her parents did not spank but sought other ways of disciplining. A few days after Christmas, she woke up from her nap. She came into the family room where her five-year-old big brother had proudly just finished putting together a puzzle he had been given for Christmas. Eyes sparkling, she walked over to the table and swept the puzzle to the floor in pieces. Then she looked up at her parents and innocently asked, "Go to my room now?" and did just that before they could even answer! Being the highly disciplined person that I am, I did not laugh at all until she was out of the room.

OUTDOOR ACTIVITY

Walter Roark advises that special bonds happen outdoors. He urges outdoor adventures starting early on: "That's the time to get them outside and sample every passable day. . . . Get them in the open air and let them shine. You'll see. Outdoor activity is a powerful antidote to built-in boredom."

He offers a "little secret": "Outside play doesn't have to be a complicated or orchestrated event." Rather it can be a simple stroll together. It can be a time to pick up souvenirs—"leaves, pebbles, aluminum cans, scraps of paper, tree bark, butterflies, insects or salamanders." The important thing is to be with each other outside, taking in the world and making memories together.

If grandparents haven't been to a playground for a while, they may be amazed to discover how magical such places can be for children, whether the equipment is simple or complex.

Gardening may be another part of a possible shared outdoor activity. Roark continues, "Toddlers and preschoolers really dig gardening. . . . Most kids have a little farmer in them, and they're ready to 'help' you whether you ask them to scatter earth, deposit seeds, plant petunias, water the roots, or pick pea pods Of course when you turn your back you might find your little helpers splashing in the birdbath, chasing butterflies or trampling your tomatoes."[8]

When my grandchildren were small, there was a large park that, along with swings and slides, had some storefronts, a jail, and other simple buildings to resemble a town in a Western movie. I remember taking a grandson there when he was five or six. He started running around in that little play village. I kept up with him for a while and then sat on a bench. Every minute or two he would appear and disappear again. All this without speaking. When we got back to the house, he told his mother all about the wild adventures he had. I had no idea!

Swimming pools can liven up a summer day, particularly if the pool has some "scary" slides. A granddaughter and I recall getting our nerve up for the highest, steepest, fastest slide. I went first, and, weighing more than two hundred pounds, made quite a splash that reached a few bystanders. My tiny granddaughter came next, barely making a ripple. But the adrenalin rush had hit both of us. We climbed the stairs and came down again and again.

At other times in winter, if there were a few inches of snow and a park with a hill or incline, we were off. Everybody who wanted could come and take what we had—a toboggan, a sled, a food tray, a piece of cardboard, anything that would slide—down the hill and up again in various combinations until we were all tired and maybe a little wet and cold. Then we went home to a fire in the fireplace and steaming cups of cocoa with lots of marshmallows. A simple joy, the stuff of memories and bonding! Other families bond over skiing and snowboarding. We enjoyed the snow, the bracing outdoor weather, and each other in our way.

SPORTS AND OTHER GAMES

Lois recalls, "We were a big sports family. Ten out of eleven of our grandkids are boys. Most of them played hockey. Lots of hockey! Playing with each other and teaching each other, participating, going to the games, following each other. We grandparents were their big fans. When hockey season was over, there was soccer and baseball. We didn't have to wonder what to do with our grandsons; there was always a game and all that goes with it."

With two of my grandchildren, the bonding sport was wiffle ball–style baseball in our backyard. This yard was a size that would mostly contain the balls from the strongest of hits. The fence around a little garden in the back provided the occasion for "out of the park" homers. Our hours of playing wore bare spots on our carefully manicured lawn, but I didn't care. They were always the batters, the home team. I was the pitcher, the visiting team, and the sportscaster narrating the game, telling of the long odds the home folk were facing. But the home team won every time—every time! The visiting pitcher saw to that.

Another grandson remembers playing basketball games with me in his backyard. His memory is that even when he was an eighth grader and 6-foot-4 (a good bit taller than me), I could still beat him in one-on-one games. (At least once. I'm sure he won most of the time.) He said that none of his school teammates' grandpas could do that. As he reflected, it increased his respect for my healthy living lifestyle.

Indoor games can be fun and enrich our lives as well. Jeanie recalls, "I noticed how good Robert, our eight-year-old grandson, was with math and told him he was ready to learn how to play euchre. Robert caught on quickly, and so my husband and I would take him along to play on euchre night at the retirement community. The others were impressed. He came to know and enjoy many more grandmas and grandpas, and they enjoy him."

My wife's family were pinochle players—there was a perpetual game of pinochle at any family reunion (only the players would change). Our children and most of our grandchildren have taken to the game. Whenever we gather, pinochle is likely to be part of our activities, with the requisite teasing, bragging, and posturing that go with any good-natured competition.

We enjoyed many board games in our home, but there were two particular favorites. One was Electronic Detective, where all the players were detectives trying to follow group and individual clues to the source of the crime, to be "rewarded" with the blaring police siren coming from the game. Very shortly after they arrived, one of the children would always go get that game and the sleuthing would begin.

The other was Mastermind. In this game of deduction and reason, one person tries to discover how the opponent has arranged four pegs of differing colors behind a barrier that hides them. How the hours flew by as we tried to find a combination that would be unsolvable and as we honed our reasoning skills.

Doug and Frieda are among the grandparents that made such game times happen over long distances. At least some of their grandchildren have always lived at a distance, for years in Hong Kong. Across vast time zones, they would arrange so that all eleven of their family could be on Zoom together to play Pictionary or Trivial Pursuit, or perhaps to celebrate a birthday, or "go to" a grandchild's violin recital or the children's Christmas pageant. Ingenuity and family triumphed!

ZEST FOR LIFE

Perhaps exuberant joy in living is what communicates the fun and celebration to our grandchildren. This was certainly true for one granddaughter who shared this memory of her Brazilian grandmother with me: "Nothing and nobody could stop grandma from having fun. She would not hesitate to go on a jet ski or motorcycle ride with one of her grandkids. Grandma would never say she was tired or too busy for anything. We traveled together a few times on long bus trips. She would fall asleep and snore loudly with her mouth open, which made us all laugh. She had a spark in her, a profound love for adventure that always stuck with me."

TRAVEL

Travel can be another way to share the fun of grandparenting. It need not be long or complicated to be enriching. Walter Roark again: "Smaller kids will grin ear to ear whenever you take them for even a short ride on a bus or train. The same is true for a taxi, subway, or ferry. To you it might be routine—to kids, these rides are a grand revelation."[9]

Recently a granddaughter and I took her two-year-old—my great-grandson—on a two-block indoor walk down to get food from the dining hall. My, what he saw on that little journey: cartoons, posters, and pictures I had ignored; fire alarm boxes; thermostats; elevator buttons to push—including the red emergency one! Not only did he enjoy it and discover many things, but I also saw my frequent routine walk through new eyes.

The grandparents with whom I spoke mentioned many memorable little journeys—on a camping trip to a state park, to a nearby city to visit a museum or go to a ball game, to visit relatives in another state with all the attractions in that new place.

Some made more extensive journeys with extended family, including grandchildren. Kathleen went on two Disney cruises with her daughter, son-in-law, and two granddaughters—the western Caribbean and the eastern Caribbean. They enjoyed a Pirate Night (splurged on the extra makeover) and had a fabulous time together. Kathleen kept a journal of each day, which sometimes helps them remember and relive that adventure.

Alan has taken his son, daughter-in-law, and grandchildren on a number of journeys. He recalls:

> Our great adventure was when we went to South Africa as a family. My late wife, Marilyn, and I had lived there two years as part of my work. I wanted my grandchildren to know a different culture. In Johannesburg, we stayed with friends who are African. They had a son the same age as my grandson, and they quickly became friends. We stayed in their home five or six days, and then we went to a game preserve together. There were many exciting sightings of animals—giraffes, two young bull elephants fighting, lions just twenty feet or so away. We met our friends again in Cape Town where we also went out to Robben Island where we saw the cell where Nelson Mandela had been a prisoner.

This was when the grandchildren were ten and seven.

Tiny or huge, simple or complex, travel opens new worlds for grandparents and grandchildren!

LAUGHING AT OUR GRANDCHILD OBSESSION

A woman was pushing her first grandchild in his stroller down Madison Avenue in New York when her husband asked her to notice what was going on: all the people were turning to look at her.

> "Of course," she said, "but they're not looking at me. They're looking at this beautiful grandchild."

> Her husband responded that they were looking at her: "You see, you are humming, and your humming is so loud."

> "What's wrong with that?"

> "Nothing, dear, but the tune you are humming is 'Hail to the Chief.'"[10]

Sometimes the joke is on us. We have to smile at ourselves, at how special our grandchildren are, at how we will listen to another grandparent's stories about theirs if they will listen to our stories about ours.

In this regard, I once wrote a limerick poking fun at myself—

> These folks they call grandp(m)as are silly;
> They boast and they brag willy-nilly.
> Such extravagant joys!
> They're just girls and boys,
> —But for one who is really a dilly!

Perhaps Rachel Naomi Remen's Orthodox Jewish rabbi grandfather struck the right note in all this. She remembers that when she was a small child, he told her many Bible stories as vividly as if he were right there. He often included the stories of women in the Bible. She recalls his telling her the story of Abraham and Sarah. As he told it, one evening when they were very old, Abraham sat outside the tent while Sarah was inside preparing dinner. Suddenly God appeared and expressed appreciation for Abraham's many years of faithful service; as a reward God would fulfill one of the wishes of Abraham's heart. Abraham stammered out that what he wanted most was a son. "Done!" was God's reply.

Inside the tent Sarah laughed at this male conversation, the ridiculous idea that at the age of one hundred, she would bear her husband a son. When God asked, "Who laughed?" Sarah said no one; "it was only the fat in the fire."

Still, months later, she gave birth a little boy. She named him Yitzak or Isaac, from the word for "laughter" in Hebrew. He was to be the beginning of a great line of teachers and wise persons.

Remen remembers being bewildered and asking, "Why does she call him Laughter, Grandpa? Is it because she laughed when God told her that he would be born?"

She remembers her grandpa's tender smile as he responded, "Perhaps, Neshume-le (his favorite term for her, meaning 'beloved little soul'). Or perhaps it is because Joy is every child's real name."[11]

As we welcome these children whose name is joy, we laugh and play with them. This is a good thing in itself—it is also the gateway to many other important callings in this grandparent vocation of ours.

FOR PERSONAL AND GROUP REFLECTION

1. Which of the activities and experiences in this chapter have you also experienced with your grandchildren?

2. Did any of the examples in the chapter contain ideas for something you might like to try with your grandchildren? If so, what?

3. What experiences of laughter and play with grandchildren have you had that were not mentioned in this chapter?

4. What about this aspect of grandparenting makes you happy? Any regrets? Any resolutions to do some new and different things? If so, what are your plans? Your first steps?

5. The chapter makes the point that laughter and play can build trust and open the door to other important grandparent conversations or other contributions. Has this happened for you? Would you like to tell about it and reflect about it?

NOTES

1. Louise Erdrich, "We Live in a Haunted Age" (interview by Hugh Delehanty), *AARP Bulletin*, November 2021.

2. Lois Wyse, *Grandchildren Are So Much Fun, I Should Have Had Them First* (New York: Crown Trade Paperbacks, 1992), 95.

3. Georgia Witkin, *The Modern Grandparent's Handbook: The Ultimate Guide to the New Rules of Grandparenting* (Thorndike, ME: Center Point Large Print, 2012), 256–57.

4. Witkin, *The Modern Grandparent's Handbook*, 260.

5. I have developed this view in some detail in my book *Laughter in a Time of Turmoil: Humor as Spiritual Practice* (Eugene, OR: Wipf and Stock, 2012).

6. Lauren Schenkman, "Meet a Scientist with a Most Enjoyable Job: He Studies Baby Laughter," TED, June 5, 2019, https://ideas.ted.com/meet-a-scientist-with-a-most-delightful-job-he-studies-baby-laughter/, accessed October 12, 2021. See also Addyman's TED Talk, "Why Babies Laugh" on this subject, available at https://www.youtube.com/watch?v=mymMye4purU.

7. Told in Loise Wyse, *You Wouldn't Believe What My Grandchild Did . . .* (Thorndike, ME: Thorndike Press, 1994), 71.

8. Walter Roark, *Keeping Your Grandkids Alive till Their Ungrateful Parents Arrive: The Guide for Fun-Loving Granddads* (Roswell, GA: Clearing Skies Press, 2004), 107–10.

9. Roark, *Keeping Your Grandkids Alive*, 109.

10. As told by Wyse, *You Wouldn't Believe What My Grandchild Did*, 32–33.

11. Rachel Naomi Remen, *My Grandfather's Blessings: Stories of Strength, Refuge, and Belonging* (Thorndike, ME: G.K. Hall, 2001), 438–39.

Chapter 6

Grandparent Presence through a Grandchild's Years (and Mine)

" For surely I know the plans I have for you, says the LORD, plans for your welfare and not for harm, to give you a future with hope."

—Jeremiah 29:11

"My grandkids believe I'm the oldest thing in the world. And after two or three hours with them, I believe it, too."

—Gene Perret[1]

When we first greet an infant grandchild, the focus is on the present moment, the wonder of a new life. It may be hard to imagine all the years, the changes, the many chapters of our relationship that will emerge. But those days come; the years roll by.

Indeed, one of the changes in grandparenting from previous generations is the length and development of our time together. And so, in this chapter we will take this long view, and we will do it in three different ways. First, we will take a brief look at the growth and development of our grandchildren from birth and over the years. There will be brief notice of our experience over those years. Second, we will reflect on the hazards and heartbreaks our grandchildren and we may encounter—some age specific, some that can happen at any time. And third, we will reflect on the grandparent response to these life changes and hazards, again from our "grandparenting as Christian vocation" perspective.

While grandparenting can begin over a wide range of ages, most typically, we are initiated with our first grandchild sometime between our mid-forties and late fifties. Barring accident or catastrophic illness, we will be grandparents for another thirty to forty years or more, nearly half our lifetimes! And we will change over that time—from midlife and active career to retirement, to early old age, to old-old. Some of that time we will be a "sandwich generation," with both parents and children and grandchildren who may need our attention and care.

Our grandchildren will experience an even more radical series of changes during those years. They will move from infant, to toddler, to school age, to teenager, to young adult, to midlife—maybe even to early retirement! This is growth and development to be celebrated. However, there will undoubtedly be crises and hazards along the way, both for our grandchildren and for us.

So let's take a look at that growth and change that is happening right before our eyes. In this chapter, we will be guided by (but not slavishly follow) the broad framework offered by Erik Erikson, a pioneering psychoanalyst and professor.[2] His gift was to broaden the focus of development from childhood alone to all of life. He pointed out that personal and social growth—and tasks—begin when we are born and continue as long as we live. His perspective was that there are eight stages of psychosocial growth over a lifetime. (Near the end of his life he and his wife, Joan, wrote there may be a ninth stage—a stage revisiting of the previous eight stages.) This gives us a framework to look at our grandchildren's development, and at ours, some decades older.

THE JOURNEY OVER TIME

The First Five Years

When our grandchildren are born, they begin an amazing and swift process of physical growth, learning, and discovery. If we continued learning and growing at the rate we do the first year of our lives, we would all be geniuses!

The growth and change continues throughout a child's early years. As a matter of fact, Erikson noted that three of the eight stages/tasks happen in a person's first five years! The first of these is "trust versus mistrust." A child arrives not knowing whether this world will be stable, nurturing, reliable, and predictable. Will the responsible adults be caring, and consistently (or at least most of the time) responsive to the child's needs? Then likely the child will develop the ability to trust and depend on relationships. While all these life tasks take place over a longer period of time and may recur later in life, Erikson saw this basically as a birth-to-eighteen-month exploration.

The second of these early childhood stages-tasks is "autonomy versus shame and doubt." This begins between eighteen months and three years or so. As a child becomes mobile and develops many physical skills, parents and other caregivers give the child some choice, allowing them to perform actions on their own. One important part of this, Erikson specifically mentioned, is potty training, developing the ability to control one's bathroom functions. Achieving this control and other physical skills, recognized and encouraged by caregivers, is so important because it makes possible the child's feeling personal power and growing independence. It is the feeling of being able to do okay in this world.

As Kathleen Stassen Berger observes, "Curious, playful, emotional, eager to explore—young children are a joy and a handful. From ages two to six, vocabulary increases by several words each day; shrieks of laughter and bursts of tears become regulated; bodies, muscles, and brain maturation enable somersaulting, cartwheeling, bicycling, tree climbing—all dependent on practice, opportunity, and guidance."[3]

Erikson's third stage of development comes in years three through five, the preschool years, and is "initiative versus guilt." In play and in family life, the child indeed takes initiative for what they want. This often runs into conflict with someone else. In play, competition, and games, a child may be assertive or even aggressive, enjoying getting their way, succeeding, or winning—but angry and frustrated when not. All of this is part of learning interpersonal skills—a task that also will go on for the rest of the child's life. The child is also learning skills and interests that help prepare them for the next big chapter of their lives.

The School Years—Ages Six to Twelve

The next block of a child's life includes elementary and the beginning of middle school. This is the setting for Erikson's stage four. His term was "industry versus inferiority." A more accurate way to phrase it might be "competence versus inferiority."

These are the years given over to basic skills—reading, writing, math. This leads to all the reasoning, discovering, and exploring that can be done when these foundational skills have been mastered.

Keeping pace with the mastery expected is important to gain the approval of important people. The child wants acceptance from teachers, to be sure, but from friends and peer groups as well. The youngster's world is growing. Succeeding in each part of this world is an urgent task.

Achieving the expected level of performance in these skills—all of them—leads to a sense of competence. Failure leads to a sense of inferiority. Indeed, there is a predictor of whether an individual will survive in the social system and avoid trouble with the law: whether, as a child, one achieves the reading and math level first taught in the first three grades at school!

Not to be ignored is the growing of people and relational skills. Indeed, well after Erikson made his observations, some have noted that fifth and sixth grade—ages ten through twelve—is the "new adolescence," with sexual maturing, fashion, dating, and all coming younger and younger, certainly into upper grade school and early middle school years.

The Adolescent Years—Ages Thirteen to Eighteen

During the middle and high school years, physical maturation continues. Bodies continue to transform from those of children into those of adults. (This does not happen uniformly—some mature early, some late). It is a time for intellectual, social, and emotional maturation to continue as well. Erikson named the psychosocial task of this period (the fifth), "identity versus role confusion."

Stassen Berger observes, "Yes, Erikson's fifth stage, *identity versus role confusion*, is evident. Adolescents struggle to establish who they are religiously, politically, and sexually; the identity crisis sometimes propels them from one set of values and behaviors to another that seems opposite to the first. That search includes words or actions that adults notice, fear, and denounce. Erikson's own children were rebellious adolescents."[4]

Kara Powell and Brad M. Griffin of the Fuller Seminary Youth Institute have done extensive and intensive research into the issues youth are facing. They note that "while every teenager is a walking bundle of questions" three questions are at the top of their concern:

- Who am I?
- Where do I fit?
- What difference can I make?

These authors note that teenagers "need caring adults willing to lean in with empathy, practice listening, and gently point them in the direction of better answers."[5] Grandparents are among these caring adults.

As classes, along with possible participation in athletic and arts activities go on, students continues to ask: What am I good at? What interests me? What doesn't? What do I value? What do I want to stand for?

For many, there will be some successes and some failures in the many topics and tasks of these years. It seems to be a human quality to take successes for granted but dwell on failures. This is certainly true for many teenagers.

For teenagers who are unsure of themselves and of preliminary answers to the questions of these years, there may be confusion about who they are and what possible futures beckon.

As Powell and Griffin note, equally compelling—perhaps even more so—is finding a group, friends, acceptance, status, and popularity with one's peers. I will never forget the bright middle high young woman who confided to me (her pastor), "I think I am smart in everything except what matters." Many will carry on much of their relating on their cell phones and various platforms. At least one possible doorway into young people's lives is through electronic communication. As part of Generation Z they are the first generation always to have had electronic devices, platforms, and means of communication.

And so pass the exciting, frustrating, confusing teenage years.

The Young Adult Years—Ages Nineteen and Beyond

The next period of a young person's life is more diffuse than Erikson's description would imply. He identified the psychosocial task (his sixth) of this age as "intimacy versus isolation." This suggests that a, if not *the*, basic task of this period is to find and form an enduring intimate relationship. That is certainly important, but it may occur much later and take different forms than Erikson envisioned when he originally wrote about this stage.

But there is so much more to the young adult journey. For the first time in life, they step "off script." Up until now, everything they do has been decided for them—mandatory schooling has been their central activity for at least the last twelve years.

Now what? Where does their discovered identity—or identity confusion—take them? University? Military service? A job? Where will they live? What will they need to survive? How will they succeed? What is their short-term and long-term plan, if any? What—if any—will their family continue to provide, and for what are they now responsible?

For some, years of college will provide some continuity—a somewhat similar schedule—to the previous twelve years. This has led to the observation that adolescence starts earlier and goes later than it has in previous generations.

And, as Erikson noted, there is the issue of exploring and searching for an enduring relationship, a partner with whom to share life. This may involve questions and experimentation about one's sexual identity. It may also include living together without marrying, for a while, or possibly permanently. It may include postponing having children or deciding against it. So begins and continues the varied and uncertain young adult journey.

Meanwhile, the Grandparent Journey

Erikson's last two stages/tasks relate to our grandparent years. His stage seven (roughly ages forty to sixty-five) is "generativity versus stagnation." A person in this life stage may want to make a contribution to those who come after them. This may be to influence, to nurture, to mentor, to encourage, or to guide. Failure to sense that one has made a difference in at least some ways may lead to sadness and disillusionment.

This desire to be generative, supportive, and helpful is not limited to one's family, of course, but it may well connect to being a grandparent. There may be many opportunities over the years to be generative with one's grandchildren.

Erikson's eighth and final stage—for those age sixty-five or so to the end of life—is "integrity versus despair." As he describes it, this is a time to reflect, to take stock, to review one's accomplishments and relationships of a lifetime. This is certainly a part of one's elder years. However, his description sounds more passive and quieter than some older adults today experience. For many of us, there is interest in being active and involved. We hope to be making contributions to the lives of our family and others to the end of our days.

Still, the years have been going by. Energy, agility, health may have taken some hits. Our relationships with our grandchildren will still be special, but they will change.

HAZARDS AND HEARTBREAKS OVER THE YEARS

The growth, development, and achievements of our grandchildren over these years are a pleasure and glory to behold. Graduations, first jobs, weddings, births, and more are causes for celebration and rejoicing.

At the same time, our grandchildren will encounter hazards and perhaps heartbreaks over these years. Some of these hazards may be in a person's own physical being. Others come from outside.

We will consider some of these possible difficulties. I warn you in advance that this is a sobering list of hazards. Furthermore, the risks are not evenly distributed. Some populations are more vulnerable. I hope you will read through and ponder this list. As compassionate persons of faith, we are part of a great sorority/fraternity of grandparents. Other grandparents and children may need our support, and we may need theirs. The welfare of all our grandchildren is a concern we share.

The First Five Years

As noted, the early years are exciting times when growth and discovery happen almost daily. But they are also years when hurt, heartbreak, or hazard can happen.

For Terry and Ruth, the heartbreak came very early. They were excited to learn that a daughter and son-in-law were pregnant with their first grandchild! However, just a couple months later, the couple came from the obstetrician's office with the sadness there was no heartbeat; the fetus was not alive. There was grieving for the child they would never know and for their daughter, who, when she was little, said she wanted to have one hundred children!

Fortunately, some time later the couple became pregnant again and carried the child to healthy birth. This little boy is much loved by all—including his grandparents.

Ron and Marge E. also experienced early heartbreak. They did not immediately go see their first granddaughter when she was born. They were hundreds of miles away, and their son, the child's father, was deployed in military service. They intended to go when he was home so they could see the whole family, but before this could happen, the little girl died of crib death. With the help of their church, Marge was able to make the difficult journey and be with their daughter-in-law, to grieve together, and to attend the child's funeral. Since then, with the birth of each grandchild, they have hastened to visit as soon as humanly possible to welcome the child and celebrate the new life in their extended family.

Though not as tragic, there are certainly other issues and needs throughout these early childhood years. One child, in his third year, was resisting all efforts at toilet training—one of the control topics Erikson mentioned specifically. His parents thought it best to let up for a while. However, just before a vacation break, he brought his parents a note from the day care center: "Do not send him back in diapers." Somehow, this issue would have to be faced and resolved for growing and learning to continue.

There are a number of special needs that may begin to appear in these first five years, and we will look at these shortly. With each, unconditional grandparent love, support, and acceptance will be so important.

The School Years, Adolescence, and Young Adulthood

There are many hazards that are not age specific or that continue over the years.

Learning Hazards

During these important years, there are a number of growth/discovery/learning hazards. A child or young person may fail to gain the skills that are foundational to future educational and occupational opportunities. There is widespread national concern about declining reading, math, and science scores. The hazard may be poor schools, or a school that is a bad fit to a particular student's way of learning.

Or it may be that the student has special learning needs. The Centers for Disease Control has published a report from their research that from 2009 to 2017 about one in six (17 percent) children aged three through seventeen years were diagnosed with a developmental disability. This was an increase from previous studies, although this may have been due to more adequate testing. The disabilities encompassed in this study included a wide variety: "attention-deficit/hyperactivity disorder, autism spectrum disorder, blindness, cerebral palsy, moderate-to-profound hearing loss, learning disability, intellectual disability. seizure in the past 12 months, stuttering or stammering in the past 12 months or any other developmental delay."[6]

One in six children and young people! The study also revealed that some children were more likely to be diagnosed with these issues—boys more than girls, non-Hispanic white or non-Hispanic Black children more than Hispanic children, and rural more than urban. All of this points to a significant minority of children—including our grandchildren—that may need attention and care to overcome learning obstacles for present happiness and future effectiveness.

Shaming and Bullying Hazard

With the importance of learning and of peer acceptance and support, there is another hazard that imperils both: shaming and bullying. This behavior comes from one's peers, where the young person most longs for acceptance and support. The bullying may be physical—fights, pinches, and slaps—or it may be interpersonal—criticism, ridicule, put-downs, gossip, and rumors. It may be direct or indirect, in person or on social media. One grandfather with whom I visited worried about his granddaughter who was quite tall and large for her age. He feared she would experience even more body shaming than had already happened.

Depression and Suicide Hazard

A hazard closely related to shaming and bullying is loneliness, self-loathing, depression, and considering—perhaps attempting—suicide. A young person may feel there is no other way out of the deep pain and unhappiness they feel.

This is a serious concern for many young people, multiplied several times over for young people who are exploring or identifying as LGBTQ+. Research reveals that these young people contemplate suicide at nearly three times the rate of non-LGBTQ+ teens. They are almost five times as likely to have attempted suicide.[7]

Family Instability Hazard

There are other hazards from outside of the growing child. A child may be in a less-than-secure home environment. Perhaps a parent or other important adult has a drinking problem, alcoholism, or a drug addiction. With or without substance use, there may be violence or abusive behavior.

This may lead to divorce, a parent dating, or remarriage. There are now more second-marriage families than first-marriage families. This requires change and adjustment for all, especially the young. Depending on who has custody, there may also be issues whether a grandparent is allowed time with the grandchildren, and how much. There have been lawsuits and legislation over grandparent visitation rights.

Sexual Harassment/Abuse Hazard

There is also the hazard of sexual harassment or abuse. A YWCA publication reports, "One in four girls and one in six boys will be sexually abused before they turn 18 years old." Ninety percent of the abusers will be known to the children—friends, acquaintances, leaders of children's groups, or family. This abuse, in turn, has tragic consequences. The YWCA reports, "Child sexual abuse can have lifetime impacts on survivors—especially without support. It can impact educational outcomes, lead to heightened symptoms of posttraumatic stress disorder, higher suicidality, drug abuse, higher likelihood of teen pregnancy and chronic health issues."[8]

Losing Loved Ones Hazard

We live in a fragile world in so many ways. All along the journey from birth to adulthood, our grandchildren can lose important people to death—perhaps a parent and, quite possibly over this time span, a grandparent or a great-grandparent. One grandmother with whom I visited worries about a grandson whose dad—her son—died. As far as she can tell, no one was available to help him grieve, remember, try to rebuild his life. He has withdrawn from family. He doesn't answer phone calls or mail, not even birthday gifts; he doesn't even cash the checks.

Drug Abuse Hazard

Another grandmother told of a grandson who did well in high school and was admitted to a highly regard church-related college of his denomination. However, he somehow became involved with drugs there and became addicted. Only very strong interventions from counselors, his home pastor, and his family succeeded in helping him overcome his addiction. Happily, he was able to return to college, graduated, found employment in his chosen career, and married. His experience exemplifies how this widespread this problem is, even where it might be least expected.

A widely accepted and used drug is alcohol. One survey reported that 80 percent of college students had abused alcohol some time and that 31 percent reported symptoms of alcohol abuse.[9]

On a related topic, nearly half (an estimated 43 percent) of college and noncollege young adults use marijuana. Whether this is viewed as simply a current practice or drug abuse, it is a fact of life that those who care about young people should be aware.

I have been citing studies about college-aged young people, but it should of course be acknowledged that these practices often are started at much younger ages.

Poverty Hazard

What does it cost to welcome a child and support that child to age eighteen? A USDA report described the increase over the years and estimated that it now costs $245,000![10] And that is before college or any other post–high school training, and whatever else may be needed before that child is established and self-supporting.

Of course, many parents of modest means will spend much less than that. They will budget so that their children can have adequate health and dental care, clothes, food and nutrition, and supplies for school. Some of the pricier lessons, music instruments, participation fees, summer camps, vacations, and so on will not be possible.

And some families—who love their children just as much—live in poverty. Health and dental care may be minimal. They may be food insecure. Preschool and other educational enrichment may be beyond their means, and the public education available to them may be in poorer school districts. Life possibilities are limited by the poverty.

Law Enforcement System Hazard

Amy, an African American grandmother, spoke with me about her grade-school-aged grandchildren: "I worry for them. There are things that are dangerous for a little Black boy or girl."

Some of the grandparents with whom I visited, particularly the African American grandparents, worried about their grandchildren's possible encounters with the police and the arrests and troubles that might follow. In connection with this, I spoke with Dr. Archie Ivy, a retired public school administrator and presently pastor of an African American congregation. I asked what counsel he gives youth and young adults in this regard.

His response: "At traffic stops, I tell them, keep your hands visible and be respectful." He relates even he—a distinguished, respected, gray-haired citizen—has been stopped and accused of speeding when he did not.

He continues, "If the person stopped has even the smallest amount of marijuana, he will likely wind up in jail. Probably he won't be able to afford bail and must remain in jail. Because of this he will probably lose his job. Then he will get arrested for lack of child support and get more jail time. Felons lose many privileges. They cannot vote, and they have a shadow over them when trying for a job. They are unlikely to have someone who will put in a good word so that they can get a job in spite of the felony."[11]

This leads to some grim prospects. As to the likelihood of ever spending time in a state or federal prison, 28.5 percent of Black men will do so. This is about twice as likely as Hispanics (16.0 percent) and 6 times more likely than whites (4.4 percent).[12] A Black youth has a stronger possibility of going to prison than going to college!

THE GRANDPARENT RESPONSE(S)

As our grandchildren grow and mature, there are many hazards! What, then, should be our grandparent response? We will have to answer this question in broad strokes. Each of us will need to invent our own strategies to whatever unique hazards our grandchildren face. Still, there are a few perspectives and observations to make.

Support the Parents

Most basically, we stand together as a family. From early on, we trust and support the parents' decisions. There is to be no criticism, second-guessing, or "triangulating" with a grandchild against the grandparents. For years, there has been a snarky and supposedly funny statement—that a reason grandparents and grandchildren get along so well is that they have a common enemy! This attitude needs to be exorcised from an extended family's life. Whatever we are facing, we stand together as a family and claim our family strength.

And the first basic step in this family strengthening is, as far as is humanly possible, to trust and support the parents' decisions and strategy in dealing with the issue at hand. State this support to the parents. Offer perspectives, suggestions, and advice only when asked—and then, only in small doses, more than matched with listening and supportiveness.

Special Needs Grandchildren

In my interviews with grandparents, I heard many stories of the needs and issues their families faced—poor eyesight or loss of eyesight, hearing problems, sports injuries, autism, Asperger's and more. The grandparents who told of these offered two essential gifts: unconditional acceptance and commitment to support over the long haul.

One grandmother told of the family learning that an internationally adopted child was diagnosed with autism at age three. While the whole family offered care, his grandpa engaged in physical play with the child, picking him up, carrying him around, tossing him up and turning him around up high—activities the child loved. Grandpa and grandchild formed a bond in that play. The child, now in high school, is nonverbal and communicates using a combination of sign language and a language of his own. But to this day, he and his grandpa have a bond. When Grandma comes to visit without Grandpa, she immediately senses his disappointment!

Another grandmother tells that her granddaughter had a series of difficulties. Finally, when she was ten, her parents' persistence resulted in the right testing and diagnosis—Asperger's. Immediately, she wanted to go and tell her grandparents. The grandmother vividly recalls that conversation. Her granddaughter began, "I have something to tell you. I have Asperger's syndrome." (Her grandmother recalls, "She sounded like a little professor telling us this.") "The doctor says said that on the spectrum, there are head bangers on one end, and I am on the other end. My brain works differently than yours." They thanked her for telling them and asked how they could be of any help.

It was a question and promise well kept. This child grew and went through unsuccessful education times and successful ones, jobs that didn't work and those that did. She finally found the right place. She was well trained for a phone answering service and has been promoted at least twice. She now has her own apartment. This was fifteen-year commitment—and of course, the story goes on.

Make Wise Financial Decisions

Still another aspect of grandparent care may involve money.

Several of the hazards mentioned may require the funds to pay for something as part of the solution. Grandparents mentioned such needs and said there must to be forethought and wisdom to how this is done. Questions need to be clarified: Is this a gift or a loan? If a gift, is it one time, or can it be repeated? If a loan, what are the terms of repayment? If it is provided to one member of the family, what are the implications for other family members?

Both for present needs and for the future, grandparents are well advised to have thought through loving and just ways to do this. They will need to discern how to use what they have for what is needed in their family and what is most important for them, personally.

Be Present, and Not Only That, a Good Listener

You may have learned the hard way what I have also learned—that advice is what we most love to give and most hate to receive!

Much more valued is simple presence: being there for the good times and the bad; listening as long as someone needs to talk or sitting in silence together if that is what is wanted and needed; asking good questions and giving honest feedback if asked; and encouraging their beginning thoughts and strategies and inviting them to explore deeper, to consider next steps.

This is the Golden Rule at work—being the person we would have loved to have when we were in the young person's shoes and offering what would have been most helpful to us back then.

It is earning the privilege of being a caring presence to the end of our days.

FOR PERSONAL AND GROUP REFLECTION

1. What of your grandchildren's growth, discoveries, and accomplishments do you most fondly remember?
2. Which of the hazards mentioned in this chapter have your grandchildren experienced? What about you?
3. In this list of hazards, what did the chapter miss?
4. What was your role in responding to any of these hazards? What went well? What did you do well? What would you do differently another time?
5. If you were writing this chapter, what would you want to tell your fellow grandparents?
6. What, if any, takeaway from this chapter do you want to hold on to, to remember, to practice? Where, if anywhere, did I get off the track?

NOTES

1. Quoted in Richard Eyre, *Being a Proactive Grandfather: How to Make a Difference* (New York: Familius, 2017).

2. Erik Erikson, *Childhood and Society*, 2nd ed, rev. and enlarged (New York: Norton, 1963). The following summary is also enriched by Jeremy Sutton, "Erik Erikson's Stages of Psychosocial Development," *Positive Psychology*, August 5, 2020, accessed October 22, 2021, https://positivepschology.com/erikson-stages/.

3. Kathleen Stassen Berger, *Grandmothering: Building Ties with Every Generation* (Lanham: Rowman & Littlefield, 2019), 149.

4. Stassen Berger, *Grandmothering*, 210–11.

5. Kara Powell and Brad M. Griffin, *3 Big Questions That Change Every Teenager: Making the Most of Your Conversations and Connections* (Grand Rapids: Baker Books, 2021), book jacket.

6. CDC, "Increase in Developmental Disability among Children in the United States," accessed October 25, 2021, https://www.cdc.gov/ncbddd/developmentaldisabilities/features/increase-in-developmental-disabilities.html.

7. Powell and Griffin, *3 Big Questions That Change Every Teenager*, 102. They in turn are citing the Trevor Project, accessed October 25, 2021, https://www.thetrevorproject.org/resources?s=Suicide.

8. YWCA, "Child Sexual Abuse Facts," September 2017, accessed October 25, 2021, https://www.ywca.org/wp-content/uploads/WWV-CSA-Fact-Sheet-Final.pdf.

9. Addiction Center, "Facts and Statistics of College Drug Abuse," accessed October 26, 2021, https://www.addictioncenter.com/college/facts-statistics-college-drug-abuse/.

10. Morgan Stanley, "When Little Geniuses Have Big Dreams," February 12, 2016, accessed October 26, 2021, https://www.morganstanley.com/articles/little-geniuses-big-dreams.

11. Dr. Archie Moore, phone conversation with the author, August 10, 2021.

12. Thomas P. Bonczar and Allen J. Beck, "Lifetime Likelihood of Going to State or Federal Prison," Bureau of Justice Statistics, March 1997, accessed October 26, 2021, https://bjs.ojp.gov/content/pub/pdf/Llgsfp.pdf.

Chapter 7

Called to Compassion for Other People's Grandkids

"Finally, beloved, whatever is true, whatever is honorable, whatever is just, whatever is pure, whatever is pleasing, whatever is commendable, if there is any excellence and if there is anything worthy of praise, think about these things."

—Philippians 4:8

"I used to think that life had four necessities: food, oxygen, love, and friendship. Now I know there's a fifth: purpose."

—Lesley Stahl[1]

As part of our calling, how and where can we grandparents offer care beyond our own families, on behalf of other people's grandchildren? What are some of us doing in this regard?

As you consider these questions, I will begin by telling of two visionary leaders who found ways to claim the gifts of grandparents to serve others. Then I will report other examples of care and service among the grandparents who visited with me and grandparents I have known. All of this is an invitation: Consider the ways of living our grandparent vocation and extending it beyond our immediate families.

DIXON CHIBANDA AND THE FRIENDSHIP BENCH

The country of Zimbabwe, like many developing nations, lacks in resources for persons with depression or other mental health issues. A few years ago, it was estimated that in this country of about 16.5 million people, there were approximately twelve psychiatrists. Obviously, they are spread very thin!

Dr. Dixon Chibanda, one of those psychiatrists, noted that a troubled young patient, Erica, had not come for her appointment. When he called to ask why, he learned that she could not afford the $15 bus fare to come to the appointment. Instead, she had committed suicide, hanging herself from the mango tree in their family garden. That was a moment of sad awakening for him.

This tragedy inspired the idea of creating an informal network of therapists throughout their land. But how would that be possible? Chibanda recalls, "After talking to colleagues, family and friends, I found out that one of the most reliable resources we have in Africa are grandmothers. They are the custodians of culture and wisdom in every community, and they don't leave their communities in search of greener pastures."[2] Further, "grandmothers are the best choice for this," he discovered, because "unlike others in the community who direct a patient what to do, they listen and guide their patients toward a solution."[3]

In spite of considerable skepticism that this would work, he set about to make it a reality. Together with Petra Mesu, he developed a training plan and therapy in the Shona language. The therapy they designed focuses on problem solving. It integrates indigenous elements with cognitive behavioral therapy.

In 2006, Chibanda trained the first fourteen grandmothers. Their method of caring-listening would be the Friendship Bench. This is an ordinary bench situated near a clinic. When troubled patients come to the health clinic for help, they may be evaluated and sent to meet a grandmother at this bench outside the clinic.

The grandmothers' training prepares them to provide six sessions of individual problem-solving therapy. It is quite informal, like talking to one's own beloved grandmother, using ordinary language. There may be need to talk of domestic violence or AIDS. The conversation may range to the concepts of *kufenisisa* (roughly translated, "if you think too much") and *kusuwisisa* (deep sadness as contrasted with normal sadness). The grandmother takes notes that are reviewed by the professional team.[4] If the patient seems suicidal, the grandmother caregiver immediately notifies her supervisor.

Patients who doe not come for their appointed time on the Friendship Bench will get a call and a follow-up, just as their own grandmother would probably do. There is no charge to the person receiving the counsel. Some of the grandmothers are modestly compensated as community mental health workers, while others donate their services.

There are now Friendship Benches in more than seventy Zimbabwean communities. Since 2006, more than 400 grandmothers have been trained. In one recent year there were 240 of these elderly community health workers at work, and more than thirty thousand people were given help as part of the project. The concept has spread to other nations as well. This treatment program has undergone objective reviews. Despite the early skepticism, it was found to be effective in fulfilling its objectives and dealing with the pain of its clients.

Chibanda reflects, "There are more than 600 million people over 65 in the world. Imagine if we could create a global network of grandmothers in every major city in the world."[5]

BRENDA KRAUSE EHEART AND HOPE MEADOWS

Lesley Stahl, a reporter for *60 Minutes*, visited Hope Meadows in Rantoul, Illinois, in 2014. She reflects that while it is unseemly—especially for a reporter—to gush, "Well, screw that when it comes to the story of Hope Meadows." Her host for the visit told her, "This is no Utopia," but noted that "by my lights it's as close as it gets."[6]

Hope Meadows is a planned community whose purpose is rescuing children who were abused, neglected, or abandoned and placing them in stable families in a safe neighborhood. This neighborhood has the added benefit of older adults who support those families and the children. It is the first of its kind, and it has served as model and inspiration for several other such communities around the country.

The founder, Dr. Brenda Krause Eheart, puts it this way: "What we're working towards is a whole new way to support vulnerable people. Another way of putting it is to really have ordinary people solve these intractable social problems—that's what it's all about."[7]

This story began in the 1990s. While studying the foster care system in Illinois, Eheart came across cases she found distressing. For example, a foster family announced they couldn't parent eight-year-old Johnny. They abandoned him at school to be picked up by a policeman and social worker he didn't know. "I couldn't stand it," Eheart says. "I had to do something."

Sometime after that, Eheart had raised enough money to purchase a subdivision of eighty houses that had been a part of the by-then-closed Chanute Air Force Base. She screened and trained potential parents to provide enduring home relationships and matched these parents with three or four children. In doing so, she tried to keep brothers and sisters together. The original group of parents were mostly couples—some white, some African American—and some single women. For this care, they were provided spacious housing, rent free. (In the early phase, if a parent stayed at home to care for the children, he or she was considered an "employee" and received a salary and health benefits. While that is no longer the case, the provision of housing continues.)

What about the grandparent component of this planned community? "It was serendipitous, a total fluke," Eheart says. Hearing about retirees who needed to downsize, she thought, why not offer retirees a three-bedroom duplex for $525 a month in exchange for six hours of volunteer work a week? She admits that her motive was simply to fill the extra forty-eight houses that had been a part of the subdivision she had purchased for this program.

The houses for these older adults are scattered throughout the subdivision. Many of them have an attached carport where the seniors who live there often sit and visit on lawn chairs. And so neighborhood children would likely walk by or ride their bicycles up into the carport. Conversations, games, snacks, treats would happen naturally. As Eheart recalls, "The seniors immediately got to know the children, and then how do you not fall in love?"

Formally and informally, the older adults serve as mentors, tutors, companions to the children, and so much more. There are game times and outings and field trips. For their required volunteer work, the older adults can do whatever appeals to them, whether tossing a ball with the youngsters, helping out in the office, or perhaps assisting with the gardening. One woman, Clarissa, who has a background in community theatre, helps with after-school activities— drama, dance and movement, or art projects.[8]

These older adults are also there for the parents who may need a helping hand, a listening ear, some time away, or a bit of respite. Many of the children have been hurt by the system and need a calm and caring but firm adult presence.

As Stahl observes, "A group of retired senior citizens—some feeling they too had been discarded—have moved there to help heal the children. But— and this was not foreseen—the children end up healing them."[9]

Wes Smith tells of Irene, one of the first older adults to move to Hope Meadows. She had been a schoolteacher but admits she had much to learn in relating to some of the troubled children living there. However, she also had a special connection. At age thirteen, she had been placed in a convent, not by her choice, but her father's. She knew a good bit about loneliness and longing! She remained a nun for thirty years, then left to become a public school teacher, and later, she married. When her husband died, she came to Hope Meadows.

The first child she encountered, Brandon, had been abused in foster care, and he had never even held a crayon. Irene welcomed him, listened to him, and smothered him with grandmotherly hugs. She also often took him with her to her family's farm, where the family also accepted him. On their first visit, two of her married nephews lifted Brandon up on a big corn picker, let him ride and even "drive" a little, and told him, "Come on, Brandon, we've got work to do!" Slowly he was coming out of his shell and calling her Grandma.

One evening at a quarter to seven, her doorbell rang. It was Brandon, holding some pennies and a dollar bill in his hand. He asked, "Grandma, may I take you to the movies?" They saw *Oliver*, and throughout the evening he would ask her if she was comfortable or if he could get her anything—her first "date" since her husband had died some thirteen years earlier.[10]

Irene reflects, "You sit here, and you watch the children, and you think, where would that child be if they weren't here in this place? And where would I be? Probably vegetating someplace if I were even still on this earth. . . . It's just so beautiful to see the little kids come here and often do a complete turnaround." At ninety, she reflects on her twenty years there and realizes those years have been her happiest. "You can put your head on the pillow at night and say, 'You know, I did help someone today.'"[11]

David and Carol Netterfield met as older adults on a Christian online dating service. They looked into Hope Meadows as a possible way to be of service. The retired couple was visiting on the front lawn of one of the families' homes when their thirteen-year-old son arrived home from school. The parents made introductions and said the Netterfields were considering moving there. "Oh good," the son said. "The apartment right beside ours is vacant. Would you move in, so we could have some grandparents?" They could not resist and did just that, becoming quite close to this family. When the mother had trouble transporting this boy to a special counselor, they provided the transportation. They would then stop to eat out afterward. They did this for about a year. They conclude, "You can guess that we were pretty well attached to him."[12]

Another grandmother, Carol, read of Hope Meadows in an airline in-flight magazine while she was a divorced mother of two working as a pediatric physical therapist in Texas. It stirred a longing in her, and when she retired eight years later, she applied and immediately came to Hope Meadows.

A trim, spry, youthful seventy-one-year-old, she became a valued addition to the community. Parents welcomed her as a back-up to parents and a resource with children. And, as one parent describes it, "All the kids line up outside her house"—to come in and play.

When asked what she got out of being at Hope Meadows, Carol responds, "I'm not here for the relationship between the seniors. I just love being around kids. I get to be a kid. . . . I know how to play. If they're in my house, I'm in the middle of the floor with them. We play games." A tent in the living room and a toy corner stacked with board games bear witness to her words.[13]

In contrast to Carol, who longed to be a part of Hope Meadows, childless Anita came reluctantly. Her husband, Maury, was drawn by the safe streets and low rent. For years, Anita continued her job as a travel agent in the city and visited only on weekends. She thought she could volunteer to do office work but not be with the children. When she visited, she was slightly surprised to see her husband actively engaged with children who called him Grandpa.

She moved in when Maury died, and the children kept coming, maybe because she kept serving them ice cream and was not upset if they spilled something. Once she "stupidly" (her word) told a child she could help with homework if he needed it, He showed up, the first of many children she helped. She also takes the children out to restaurants when one of her crowd of young friends has a birthday. Another of her activities is to lead groups of children on trips to Chicago to visit a museum or to shop. Though her husband chose this life for her, she appears to be enjoying it tremendously and is not lonely or bored, and certainly not isolated.

These surrogate grandparents are enriched by the purpose they find in their lives. It even contributes to their physical health. George King had come in frail health, depressed and moody. His health was so tenuous that he had a home health nurse. He had been told that he probably only had a year more to live. Caring for the children, including the most damaged among them, was invigorating for George. After three months, he told his nurse not to come any more. And instead of living just another year, he thrived and lasted another fifteen years.[14]

Over and again, among these caring surrogate grandparents it has proven true that "it is one of this community's blessings that the healing works both ways. . . . The seniors accept the children as they come to them, and the young respond in kind."[15]

THE STORIES I HEARD

I asked the grandparents I interviewed if they had done any volunteerism projects as grandparents—for their own or other people's grandchildren. Here are some of the stories I heard.

Caring Grandparents

Ann reached out with friendship and interest to a couple with two young boys in her church. Their extended family was some distance away. Occasionally, she was asked to care for the two boys when both parents had to be gone. Other times, she cared for one of the boys when the parents took the other for medical evaluations or school appointments. Also, when children in her neighborhood learned from home during the COVID epidemic, they would visit, masked, over the back fence, and they would bring her pictures. And when a Burmese family with a school-aged daughter stayed in her church's "mission house," she often transported the child to school and back, as the family had no car. A warm adult-child friendship developed. Ann was also part of child enrichment and vacation church school that her church offered.

Many of the other grandparents also spoke of their involvement in educational and missional efforts with children and youth at their church as part of their commitment. With Carl and Mary Ann R., her involvement was with preschool children; his, with youth—in church school, youth group, mission trips. "We want the church to be strong and to be there for next generations," they told me. This perspective was shared by Ron and Carol S. While she is a kindergarten public school teacher, they enjoy teaching the fifth and sixth graders: "They are thinking for themselves and ask good questions," which they enjoy engaging.

Each year, at least one Sunday morning, Ron and Carol lead this class in baking bread, filling the church with tantalizing smells and having delicious biscuits out for any who want a taste. Children look forward to being in their class and making bread. Ron also connects the children's energy to helping them find a place to use that energy. For example, he introduced a lively pair of twins to the church's head usher. The boys now faithfully serve on the usher team.

Each summer, Carol creates a special week of some activity for church and neighborhood children. From her experience of increasingly having Muslim children in her public school class, she had an idea. One year, she created that week to be one of interfaith encounter and learning between children and parents of these two faith traditions. She is considering making the curriculum she created available to others.

Doug and Frieda S. channel their desire for a better world for their grandchildren into involvement in local politics. They identify candidates who stand for what they believe, and actively campaign for those persons. They also told me, "This last year we participated in Black Lives Matter events with our granddaughters. They have a lot of friends of different races. All these issues are important to them and to their friends."

Kathy told me, "When my daughter taught kindergarten, I was the grandparent in the classroom, helping those who were having the most difficulty learning to read. I loved that experience; my background is in education. The children would say to me with wonder, 'Mrs. B., you are our teacher's mother!'"

Kathleen supports all the fund raisers for her granddaughters' parochial school. She confesses this involves a good bit of buying and giving.

As long as he was able in his retirement years, Bob volunteered at a community food pantry, and he also drove for Meals on Wheels. He saw this as a continuation of the way his family lived, contributing to a strong community. It was also a subtle witness to his granddaughters, that "this is who our family is, and this is what our family does."

Out of her concern for children's well-being and educational problems, Amy served on the school board in her city for a number of years. She also gave leadership in creating a place of temporary housing, care, and mentoring for homeless students. She was dismayed to find this need, where in addition to all the other problems of homelessness, students' participation in their education suffered.

Margy, a retired art teacher, found many ways to be of service. She told me, "I volunteered at University Children's Hospital. There is an activity room. What I liked to do was art projects with them, either in their rooms or in this activity room. I was also in the first class of volunteers at the Chazen Museum of Art. I gave tours there so many years. I also participated in Very Special Arts USA. I volunteered, assisting in art classes for children with various disability issues, children of all ages. It's a rewarding thing to volunteer, rewarding for me."

She continued, "My husband and I also participated in an Alzheimer's research study. (We did not suffer from that disease.) Twice a year, we would go spend seven to eight hours doing blood tests as well as verbal and written tests."

Stephen Ministers

As I read about the grandmas offering caring-listening on Friendship Benches, I felt a nudge of recognition. In a modest way, I had been a part of something like that. I had also seen grandparents exercising these gifts.

For a number of years when I was a pastor, I led a Stephen Ministry[16] program in my church. This is a nationally franchised nonprofit program out of St. Louis, Missouri. Stephen Leaders, trained by this organization recruit, train, and provide group supervision to Stephen Ministers, who are lay people. There is a year of training in lay ministry/Christian listening/caregiving. Then the Stephen Minister serves for at least a year offering weekly one-on-one caring, listening, and support to a person assigned to them. This care receiver may be lonely, grieving, overwhelmed, discouraged, depressed, or have some other need.

I remember a number of the grandparents that I recruited and trained to be Stephen Ministers/Christian caregivers. Gratefully, I recall all the energy and creativity they brought to the persons I asked them to care for.

One grandmother—let's call her Olive—was assigned a single mother who was feeling overwhelmed with her preschool-aged child and caring for her home. When Olive called to make an appointment, this young mother said she would love to have someone to talk with but would not let anyone come into her messy house! Fine, Olive said, how about if we set a time and talk on the phone? The young mother agreed, and they did that for a year. She felt supported, time and again. Further, she never had to endure the embarrassment of someone seeing how she kept their home.

Another, call her Rita, was also assigned an overwhelmed single mother. She had to be creative and adaptable as well. This mother's work schedule as a waitress with varying shifts at two restaurants was erratic. So it was hard to schedule. Further, her young and very energetic son was always with her when she was not working. Okay, Rita said, let's find a time and a playground. We will sit on a bench and talk while your son plays. Here was a person who desperately needed a friend but whose schedule didn't make it easy! Rita continued to be nimble to be that friend.

I think of another, let's call her Grace, who answered a very difficult assignment I asked her to take. Once in a while, a call would come from another church with Stephen Ministry asking if we would extend care to someone who had moved to our community. I had one of those calls.

They told me that a family who had moved near us had just experienced a suicide in their family. Did I have anyone who had experienced the suicide of a family member and could call and go spend time with them? I did. Years before, Grace's son had committed suicide as well.

I asked her, and she made the call. She went and spent time with the family as together they suffered and grieved through this most difficult of all bereavements.

I remember still another, Maxine. She served the year as Stephen Minister to people in our church and community. Then she spent two days a week for the next fifteen years as a volunteer lay assistant chaplain in a huge university hospital. She spent those years walking the halls, calling on assigned patients, listening to them, and praying with them. Only in her late eighties, when she could no longer walk the long halls, did she reluctantly give it up.

She also served with me as part of a team recruited by a chaplain at a women's prison. The chaplain asked us to come and train and give support to a group of women prison inmates. We were to train them to serve as "Caring Friends," somewhat similar to Stephen Ministers, with their hurting fellow inmates. As we had the rare privilege of being allowed to bring in some refreshments for these training and support sessions, Maxine made huge batches of a wide variety of homemade cookies. This was such a beloved treat to these women who had to live on bland prison food. It was hard to know which they treasured more, Maxine's presentations or her cookies!

AND SO—

None of the people I mentioned thought they were doing all that much or anything special. Most strained to remember what they had done. Many felt they could have done more. And yet each had their impact. And there are countless struggling children, overwhelmed families, and undersupported community agencies that could benefit from more people like them.

Their stories stir a question for each grandparent: What does my love for my grandchildren propel me to do for other people's grandchildren and for the world in which they live? What is my calling?

FOR PERSONAL AND GROUP REFLECTION

1. Which, if any, of the stories in this chapter stirred memories of people you know—grandparents and other older adults doing creative and helpful things in their elder years?
2. What activities have you engaged on behalf of your own and other people's grandchildren or other community needs?
3. What nudges or invitations did you hear in this chapter?
4. What are you most concerned about as regards your grandchildren's present and future welfare? What have you done about it? What can you do about it?
5. What connections do you make between the stories in this chapter and your calling as a Christian grandparent?

NOTES

1. Lesley Stahl, *Becoming Grandma: The Joys and Science of the New Grandparenting* (New York: Blue Rider Press, 2016), 208.

2. "Dixon Chibanda—The Friendship Bench," Hearts on Fire, accessed November 2, 2021, https://www.heartsonfire.org/dixon-chibanda.

3. Evan Shapiro, "How Zimbabwean Grandmothers Are Stepping in to Fight Depression," *Time*, February 7, 2019, accessed November 2, 2021, https://time.com /5523806/friendship-bench-zimbabwe-mental-illness/.

4. "Dixon Chibanda," *Wikipedia*, accessed November 2, 2021, https://de.wikipedia .org/wiki/Dixon_Chibanda.

5. "Dixon Chibanda—The Friendship Bench."

6. Stahl, *Becoming Grandma*, 199–200.

7. Quoted in Beth Baker, *With a Little Help from Our Friends: Creating Community as We Grow Older* (Nashville: Vanderbilt University Press, 2014), 99.

8. Baker, *With a Little Help from Our Friends*, 101–102.

9. Stahl, *Becoming Grandma*, 200.

10. Wes Smith, *Hope Meadows: Real-Life Stories of Healing and Caring from an Inspiring Community* (New York: Berkley Books, 2001), 49–50.

11. Stahl, *Becoming Grandma*, 203, 206.

12. Baker, *With a Little Help from Our Friends*, 102.

13. Stahl, *Becoming Grandma*, 217.

14. Stahl, *Becoming Grandma*, 213, 214.

15. Smith, *Hope Meadows*, 58.

16. Stephen Ministries website, https://www.stephenministries.org/default.cfm.

Chapter 8

The Call to be Parent to One's Children's Children

"Religion that is pure and undefiled before God, the Father-Mother is this: to care for orphans and widows in their distress."

—James 1:27a, An Inclusive Version

"Grandparents having to step in to raise their grandchildren is an enormous issue that permeates every segment of society, yet it is barely on anyone's radar screen."

—Deborah Doucette[1]

In doing the reading for this book, I came across a term I hadn't seen before—*alloparenting*. The word *allo* comes from the Greek word for "other." Michaeleen Doucleff studied this subject and observed alloparenting in widely divergent ancient cultures. Along with her preschool daughter, she visited families among the Mayan (on the Yucatan Peninsula in Mexico), Inuit (in the Arctic village of Kugaaruk in Northern Canada), and Hadzabe (in Tanzania) cultures.

She points out that alloparenting points to a richer practice than the term might seem to imply. It does not refer to a side or minor role in a child's life: "Oh, no. They're central, omnipresent sources of love and care for children, responsible for much more than changing diapers or rocking a baby to sleep."[2]

From infancy on in the ancient cultures she observes, a large group of persons—neighbors, friends, family, relatives, and even older children—all share in the supervision and care for the welfare of the children. As one Hadzabe mother, Subion, told Michaeleen, "Ultimately, you are responsible for your own children, but you have to love all the children like your own."[3]

Doucleff contrasts this to her contemporary American experience—she and her husband, novices to infants and parenthood, were essentially on their own. They struggled with the exhausting and sometimes puzzling task of being, for the most part, the only responsible adults for their infant daughter. The wisdom she saw in these ancient cultures, including but not limited to alloparenting, felt very wise and inviting to her.

Those who write on this subject sometimes include grandparents among the alloparents, sometimes not. However, as I explore the topic of this chapter, I see grandparents who are alloparents and grandparents who need alloparents!

GRANDPARENTS AS ALLOPARENTS— GENEROUS BUT NOT TOTAL

I discovered a number of grandparents serving as alloparents. They are providing significant but partial care to their children's children. Here are three of the stories.

Dale and Nancy

I visited with two friends of mine about their alloparenting as grandparents. Let's call them Dale and Nancy.

Dale and Nancy's involvement in parenting began when granddaughter Bonny was only a year and a half old. Bonny's parents divorced, and Bonny and her father (Dale and Nancy's son) moved into their basement, even as their son's drinking problem was worsening. While he tried to be a good parent, it often fell to Dale and Nancy to be sure Bonny was safe, fed, provided for. They also took her to Sunday school with them. Over the years, with their example and faithful church participation, she made a best friend at church. Accompanying her grandparents, she was also active at their church. Over the years she was part of the church's preschool, choirs, children and youth activities, church camps, and mission trips.

Bonny's mother moved to a different community two hours away, and Bonny attended middle and high school there. In those years, Dale and Nancy would travel down for her basketball, volleyball and gymnastics events. They would also meet the mother halfway on the weekends that Bonny was to be with them.

When it was time to think of college, her parents did not help her with college or scholarship applications. Again, Dale and Nancy stepped in with guidance and financial support to help her get started.

In time, her parents addressed their problems. Bonny's dad overcame his drinking issues after another trip through rehab and follow-up programs. By this time, Bonny was a competent young adult, thanks to her grandparents, who were there for her at every turn.

She is now an educator (like her grandparents), married, the mother of two, and doing well. When Dale and Nancy complimented Bonny on all she had accomplished, she responded that she could not have done it without them. While she would have liked presence and support of her parents, she said, "I had you." That, they said, made it all worth it.

Ron M. and Susan P.

Ron and Susan had a unique opportunity to help. Their son Jesse and his wife, Cindy, were establishing themselves with a popular food truck in Memphis, Tennessee, as the pandemic came. Food trucks do well during such times, but childcare was wiped out by the pandemic. And so these two grandparents support their son's work by providing care for their two children, three days a week.

Ron reflects, "My son Jesse has found his niche. He is a tremendous manager, excellent cook, and, according to newspaper polls, the number-one food truck in the city. We are helping Jesse do what he is called to do. He hires people, trains them to be higher functioning people by being a good boss. By caring for his children, we are an integral part of that."

Both Ron and Susan are trained in early childhood education and other caregiving skills. Still, in the day-to-day care of children ages four and seven, there are obstacles. Ron reflects, "When you are with the children all day long, you become an object of rebellion. It is almost easier to be grandparent three or four times a year. Our challenge is to stay on top of it and find ways to 'melt their rebellious hearts.'"

These grandparents support parents in building a good business and rending ministry while doing it. The parents know their children are certainly not suffering from neglect, but instead are being cared for by two wise and gentle people—their own grandparents. Further, grandparents and children build memories together. Each day Ron writes down things he heard the children say, and he will treasure those sayings years from now. It is a win-win all around, even if somewhat draining on the sixty-something grandparents some days.

Ron and Carol S.

Two years ago, when their daughter went through a divorce, she and her three sons moved in with her parents, Ron and Carol. Mother and sons are living with them as she gets back on her feet. When their daughter is working, they provide care and supervision for the children. On workdays, they pick up the boys from preschool and school. They prepare meals for the whole group, do bedtime routines, and just fill in when their daughter can't do it or feels overwhelmed.

"We don't have the privacy of living alone in our house. There are always clothes and such lying around," they tell me. "It's a lot like when our kids were little. But now it is part-time. The good thing is knowing that these boys are being taken care of and that they are fed, warm, and loved. It is a trade-off for us. We don't have to fight for this privilege." On the evening I visited with them, one of the boys had helped Ron cook supper and was very proud of having done so. He wanted to do it again.

What about discipline? "They are pretty good about our disciplining. We and our daughter have similar parenting styles. They get the same answer whomever they go to. They might not like the answer, but at least we are all on the same page."

They also have a granddaughter, their son's daughter, now twelve, whom they have given much care from her birth on. She is in and out of their home a few times a week and sometimes stays overnight with them. In every way, they are active partners and support in the lives of their grandchildren.

GRANDPARENTS WHO MIGHT NEED ALLOPARENTS: SERVING AS PARENTS OF THEIR CHILDREN'S CHILDREN

There is another group of grandparents who are providing even more—all of the care for one or more of their grandchildren. They will do so for the foreseeable future. Often, they do this with limited resources.

Who Are They? How Many? How Did They Wind up as Parents?

These are persons who are taking responsibility for raising/parenting a child or children of their children. Almost always, the decision to do this is precipitated by a crisis or a tragedy. It is not just an issue for any one racial or ethnic group and is not confined to the urban poor.

Sylvie de Toledo writes, "Parenting a grandchild is a necessity born of tragedy, and tragedy has no regard for location, ethnicity, religion, class, or race. Grandparenting is color-blind. It is also class-blind."[4]

There are a number of ways this happens. Deborah Doucette's collegiate daughter did not know that antibiotics mitigated the effectiveness of her birth control, and she became pregnant shortly before breaking up with her boyfriend. Doucette knew her daughter was not temperamentally open to parenthood. She also knew that she would not let this child out of her family. So she became a very young grandparent-parent when her youngest child was just a few years older than this new addition.[5]

There are a number of reasons that bring this crisis need of parenting a child to a grandparent. Among them are:

- Alcoholism or other drug addiction and abuse (observers note this is a frequent and growing problem),
- Unplanned and unwanted pregnancy,
- Child endangerment, abuse, or abandonment,
- Domestic abuse, divorce, or separation,
- Incarceration (of the 1.5 million adults incarcerated in state or federal facilities, more than half have at least one child under age eighteen),[6]
- A birth parent's mental disorder or other disability,
- The death of one or both of a child's birth parents, and
- Military deployment of a single parent.

While we certainly wish these conditions did not exist, they are not the fault of the child! When one of these crises happens, either the children wind up in the social welfare system for foster home or institutional placement, or a family member steps in and provides home and family for the children.

About seven-eighths of these providers are grandmothers. A much smaller percent are two grandparents together or a grandfather.

While this can happen at any grandparent age, one rough estimate is that one-third of grandparents providing this care are under age fifty-five, one-third are between fifty-five and sixty-four, and one-third are sixty-five or older. This additional responsibility of childcare comes to some grandparents who are still employed and to others in their elder years, often with diminishing health and energy.

While these circumstances happen to people of all social classes, the experience is much harsher for those who are poor and have limited resources. The National Council on Aging notes that almost 75 percent of Social Security recipients depend on this source for all or most of their income, approximately $15,000 a year, and that more than 23 million Americans aged sixty and above are economically insecure, defined as at or below 250 percent of the federal poverty level. This translates to $28,725 for a single person.[7]

How many grandparents as parents are there? This question admits to no ready answer. The exact circumstance of full-time and long-term grandparenting as parenting is hard to extract from census data. Doucette, citing one census source, states, "There are 2.7 million grandparents raising 5.4 million grandchildren in the United States alone. Other countries . . . are also struggling."[8] The back cover of another book on this subject contends, "According to the US Census Bureau, 10% of all grandparents in the nation are raising their grandchildren, and the number is going up."[9]

On the other hand, psychology professor Kathleen Stassen Berger cautions about the careless reading of some census statistics. Her analysis notes that "in the United States, only one grandmother in two hundred is custodial. . . . Only about one household in four hundred has a grandmother who has been sole caregiver for five years or more."[10] These authors all agree that however many there are, grandparents as parents deserve much more attention, care, and support than is currently provided.

This is a family type that now has its own developing description and vocabulary, for example,

- Grandfamily (a family unit in which one or two grandparents is head of the household actively parenting the grandchildren),
- GRG (grandparents raising grandkids),
- GAP (grandparents as parents),
- skipped generation, and
- kinship care (as a category in the foster care system).

Certainly, within our sorority/fraternity of grandparents, this group of us with heavier responsibilities deserves the attention and support of the rest of us. That is the purpose of this chapter.

What Are Their Initial Tasks?

As Kenneth Doka notes, when a grandchild needing parental care comes on the scene, almost always from some form of loss, "one's sense of an assumptive world is challenged. This is not the way it [life] is supposed to be."[11]

While struggling to adapt to the new reality, there is a child or children with many needs in the grandparent's care. This grandchild's basic needs fall into three groups: physical, mental, and spiritual.

The physical needs include nutritious food and a safe place to live. Of course, this includes a bed and private space if possible. It also means eventual, and perhaps immediate, dental and medical care.

Mental needs might start with enrolling the child in school and giving attention to any learning deficits that might have happened during the events leading up to the child's arrival. Other mental needs include learning to live in their new world and their new reality. They may need to be given extra praise and recognition. They also need to be honored for who they are and how they are doing. Further, they may need help with problem solving, discovering interests, and exploring their new world.

And whatever the reason that the child is in a grandparent's care, they need to be reassured that they are loved. As part of this, they also need to experience consistent, dependable care.[12] Perhaps this was missing from their previous life.

Further, a committed grandparent will give attention to the child's spiritual and religious life. This may mean the grandparent introduces the child into his or her faith community, helping people know the child and helping child feel at home and welcome there. Prayer at meals and bedtime might be introduced. Bible story books might be added to story times.

There may need to be a different approach if the birth parents are of a different religion or none and if that is what they continue to want for their child. It may boil down to the grandparent living a life of faith and integrity with love for the grandchildren living in the home.

There are also a number of issues/tasks to address in a state's social system of monitoring childcare and welfare. One has to do with custody. There are two kinds of custody—physical (the child lives with you) and legal (authority to make decisions regarding the medical, educational, health, and welfare needs, and more, of the child).[13] Some grandparents may have a very informal custody. Others may need to work with an attorney or social worker to obtain both kinds of custody, which they may need in order to be able to act on the child's best interests.

Careful record keeping and document collecting is also a wise early and continuing practice. The record keeping has a twofold purpose. One is to keep organized track (including addresses and phone numbers) of persons—attorneys, social and welfare workers, teachers, school counselors, and more—connected to the grandchild.

Another part of record keeping is to be ready to be an advocate for the child. As the one constantly with the grandchild, the grandparent is more aware of the child's issues and needs. This might include information about interactions with birth parents and the impact on the child. The more informed and equipped with accurate information, the better the possibility that the grandparent's advocacy will have the desired result.

In this connection, wise practice includes collecting and maintaining many documents that may be needed along the way. This includes birth certificates, the birth parents' divorce papers, the grandchildren's Social Security numbers, medical and dental records, power of attorney, guardianship or adoption papers, school records and report cards, and undoubtedly much more.[14]

Another task is to begin dealing with financial issues. Raising children, providing for their needs, rearranging living space, and more is expensive! Almost one-fifth of grandparents raising their grandchildren have income below the poverty level. Again, de Toledo counsels that whatever obligations one feels for a grandchild, "you do not have an obligation to support them financially. Financial support is a parent's responsibility and if parents don't fulfill that responsibility, their children are entitled to government assistance."[15] Whether grandparents decides to access this potential government assistance or pay all the expenses themselves, there are decisions and adjustments to make.

All this is needed as grandparents experience the shock and endure the chaos of coming together into one household.

What Are Their Issues and Struggles?

Going through the process just described takes its toll. Rae Simons notes that grandparents as parents are vulnerable to a range of problems that include depression, loneliness, poverty, and poor health.[16]

Stassen Berger reports that the longer grandmothers have total responsibility for their grandchildren, the worse their health becomes: "Custodial grandmothers have 'generally poor physical and mental health,' 'intense stress and depression,' uncontrolled diabetes and high blood pressure. Vacations, nutrition, and sleep suffer."[17] Of course, she and the authorities she is quoting are summarizing trends, not what happens to every custodial grandparent.

The loneliness and isolation can be overwhelming. Harriet Hodgson reflects, "Loneliness walked in the door when your grandchild walked in the door."[18] No one intends this, certainly not the vulnerable grandchild or the grandparent. But the number of tasks to be done leave little spare time, making custodial grandparents so busy that friends may stop inviting them to lunch, coffee, bowling, or other events.

The all-consuming day-to-day tasks may mean custodial grandparents have little in common with friends who have a wide range of leisure interests and travel experiences. Well-meaning friends may not know how to be available, and custodial grandparents may not know how to ask. Hodgson goes on, "As time passes, grandparenting can make you feel trapped, with no end in sight. . . . Loneliness can lead to the blues, and the blues can lead to depression, a real medical illness."[19]

There is likely another emotion at work that complicates this grandparent journey—guilt, perhaps experienced as regret or self-blame. Some call guilt "A Monster in the Room."[20] Custodial grandparents may feel somewhat guilty or responsible for whatever calamity led to their grandchildren's displacement. There may also be a sense that they are not being a very good parent to their grandchildren. They may feel they are not preparing delicious meals, not being patient enough, not being understanding enough, losing one's temper, and so on.

At the same time, the grandchildren may be feeling responsible and therefore guilty for what went wrong in the home of their birth. They may feel if they had been a better child, all this would not have happened.

Along with the guilt, there may be anger. This may include anger at fate, at the courts and family welfare system, at the adult children whose lapses brought this about. For the older of us grandparents, it may be difficult to recognize, admit, and seek counsel for the anger bubbling below the surface.

These are damaging, irrational, but completely understandable emotions. Perhaps a conversation with a trusted friend, religious caregiver, or medical adviser will help. Or a support group may provide perspective—which will be discussed in more depth later.

Grandparents as parents may also experience fear—fear that they will not be allowed to keep their grandchildren in their care, fear that they will not be up to the task, fear that their health will not sustain them for as long as they are needed. There may also be doubt: Did I do the right thing? Is this fair to the grandchild? Am I up to this task?[21]

It should be no surprise that, as de Toledo describes it, grandparents as parents find themselves on an emotional roller coaster! She writes, "On any given day [these grandparents] can go through a full spectrum of feelings; grief and shame for their grown children, love for their grandchildren, fear for a future in which their health and finances may dwindle, resentment at a juvenile courts system that treats them with disrespect, anger at losing their dreams at this time of their lives, and guilt for feeling that anger."[22]

What Are the Rewards? The Unresolved Issues?

Recently I visited with a grandmother serving as mother—let's call her Meri—and heard her story. Years ago, her daughter "just wasn't mentally able to care for her children." She reported the lack of parenting, and the children were removed from that home. It took some time for Meri to win the trust of the social worker managing their case, but eventually she was awarded custody of the three children, two boys and a girl. She provided a home and cared for them for almost ten years. By then, her daughter was doing better, and was perhaps more able to deal with energetic teenagers, and so, by mutual agreement, the young people were returned to the daughter's custody.

Later, a little girl—a great-grandchild—was born to one of those grandsons and his partner at the time. One time when Meri was caring for her, she saw welts on her legs and learned her mother had beaten her with a belt. She took the child to a hospital for evaluation. The little girl was taken from her mother and put in Meri's care. She has had this child, her great-granddaughter, for much of the child's life, and she is now seven. Meri receives modest financial support for providing kinship care in the family welfare system. Now in her seventies, she also works twenty to thirty hours a week clerking at a grocery store. Earlier, she had a stroke, but doesn't think the children had anything to do with that. She feels she is in pretty good health and hopes to care for this little girl well into the future.

I asked her the hardest and best part of her parenting as a grandparent. "The hardest part was getting them and taking them away from my daughter," she told me. "The best part was seeing their faces every day, seeing them grow and prosper. Getting them involved in basketball and soccer, that was the best." She still sees these grandchildren often, and they are supportive and helpful to her, solicitous if she is sick.

I asked what Meri would like other grandparents to know about being parent to one's children's children, and their children. She answered, "How much joy a child can bring into your life. They bring light and life and a whole bunch of love into your life. There's nothing I love better than taking care of this little girl and helping out at the food pantry at the church. Nothing is more important than this for me. This is who I am."

I also learned of the experience of another grandmother, now sixty-nine years old. Let's call her Ginger. Ginger is a former educator in the public school system. She and her husband have two adult children. Their daughter had a child, a little boy, during her first year of college. She was suffering from bipolar disorder and was also dealing with addiction issues. Their attempts to help their daughter be a responsible parent proved unsuccessful. So they took both their daughter and their grandson into their home. These grandparents found themselves caring for the little boy most of the time, as the mother was intermittently gone starting when the child was less than a year old.

Then Ginger was diagnosed with lymphoma. She had to resign her school position and go on disability. At about this time, they adopted this grandson. Through health and illness, they provided his full-time constant care. Their child, the boy's mother, was in and out of the home and the boy's life inconsistently.

This boy is now seventeen, and he clings to his mother no matter how bad things are. The grandmother, who has been there for him all these years, often feels like the person less appreciated in this family picture. Theirs is a family, like many grandparent-as-parent families, with unresolved issues, and the story is not yet complete.

What draws grandparents into this complicated process that has so many crises, tangled relationships, and needy children involved? Anne E. Streaty Wimberly responds, "Intercessory hope is the grandparents' act of standing with and for their grandchildren in the parents' stead." They do this "in order to make possible for their grandchildren a worthwhile present and future life." As one grandparent told her, she was "stumbling forward in the thick of things anyhow even though I don't know how it's gonna turn out."[23]

Deborah Doucette, who raised her granddaughter and advocates for grandparents as parents, writes, "Grandparents long for, pray for, and fight for three things: to keep their grandchildren safe; to see their adult children come through their bad times to emerge as healthy, responsible people; and to come together as a family, healed and whole."[24]

At the end of her book about these grandparent-as-parent journeys, she reflects. She says she wanted to hear that it was wonderful to be raised by grandparents and that children's hearts can be without scars. However, she knows that there is no simple "happily ever after." She also knows that "raising emotionally secure children is so very difficult," that desired outcomes are not certain, and that the work is never truly finished.

Nevertheless, she concludes "that there is nothing I can do that is more important than keeping my family together, and that I am blessed to have my family intact and moving forward toward the future. There is room in my heart for all these things."[25]

GRANDPARENTS AS ALLOPARENTS TO OTHER GRANDPARENTS

What do grandparents as parents need from us grandparents with lesser responsibilities? Perhaps some of us are called to be "allograndparents"—to coin a new word. When we make that offer, that commitment, there are many possibilities.

Support the Search for a Support Group

One clear answer was offered by the grandparent-parents whose stories I have been telling. They spoke of the great relief and hope they felt the first time they attended a grandparent-as-parent support group.

And so, for any who are just entering into this new parenting venture, finding and attending such a support group may be literally lifesaving! There may be a local group to attend in person or an online group in which they can participate. If new grandparent-parents do not know how significant this can be, it is important to encourage this. If they don't know where or how to find a group, any guidance, direction, or coaching that facilitates this will be helpful. If they need childcare, or a ride, it will be good to provide that.

The knowledge that they are not alone with all these responsibilities, the company of others who are going through similar struggles, the shared discoveries about rights, resources, and helps—all this and more might be in the mix.

How might such a group be found? Sylvie de Toledo suggests going to the internet and search for "grandparents as parents" or "grandparents raising grandchildren" and add the word "meetings."[26] Or one might contact state or county agencies on the aging, the American Association of Retired Persons (AARP), or a council on aging.

The importance of finding such a support group cannot be overemphasized. At the same time, it is probably wise also to heed a caveat offered by Andrew Adesman and Cristine Adamec, that an occasional support group can become "complaints sessions that focus on the adult children's problems, rather than discussing how situations can improve." They admit a little complaining is normal, but if more than half of it is complaint, perhaps another group should be sought.[27]

Not-So-Simple Friendship

As we noted, many grandparent-parents speak of their loneliness, absorbed in the many demands of raising their grandchildren. Old friendships seem to disappear because they no longer have time for a leisurely luncheon, outing, or shopping trip. Friendship that fits their needs might be welcome. This might involve coming to them; fitting their schedule; bringing the beverages, snacks, or lunch; listening; supporting; helping out in some tasks at hand; and being together.

Respite Care

There may be a need for someone to be with the grandchildren so custodial grandparents can run errands, go to medical and other appointments, or meet with the school counselor. As the grandparent-parenting process begins, this may be a new need with no apparent solution. Stepping into this gap with offers to stay with the children may be a valuable gift.

Friendship, Tutoring, Guidance for the Child

Children may have experienced some learning lapses or gaps before arriving at their grandparent's home. Perhaps tutoring to help them feel caught up and at pace with other students may be a lift. Or children may have loneliness or anger or behavioral issues and need some one-on-one attention.

And beyond any particular issue, alloparents simply know, like, and care about each other's children. Allograndparents can do the same. Getting to know the children, reading a book together, learning a new game, taking the dog for a walk together, going to a museum, taking in a movie, playing ball or watching a ball game—any such activities can extend the caring community and family feel for grandparents and children alike.

Support in Financial and Legal Issues

Some among the allograndparents may have experience dealing with the social welfare system and the legal maze that the grandparent-parents must traverse. This may involve coaching, locating reasonably priced professional help, accompanying them, or whatever else is needed.

Adequate Housing

Adequate housing may be a hard issue for grandparents raising children. If they live in housing designated for older adults, they may be no longer eligible if minor children move in with them. Or they may live in a small apartment that was adequate for one or two people living alone but not so when their grandchildren move in.

There has been a beginning response to this need that needs to multiply and expand. In 2004, the city of New York funded and constructed the fifty-unit Grandparent Family Apartments in the South Bronx. Managing this complex is a joint effort among Presbyterian Senior Services, the West Side Federation for Senior and Supportive Housing, and the New York City Housing Authority.

In these apartments a variety of services are offered for the grandparents, including legal assistance, transportation, mental health care, parenting classes, support groups, and excursions and outings. For the children and young people, there are after-school programs and tutoring. These services are essential for such a housing complex to succeed in providing safe, healthful care and support to these families.

Further, the residents and their grandchildren offer much support to each other. Megan Dolbin-MacNab, an associate professor in Virginia Tech's Department of Human Development and Family Science, notes, "You're putting people together who have similar experiences and needs and providing them with a sense of community." These grandparent residents have the opportunity, often claimed, to become allograndparents for each other.

Of course, the need for such a place far exceeds the available apartments. There is a long waiting list. And there are eligibility requirements of age, income not beyond a certain range (20 percent of which will be paid in rent). And the grandparents will have to leave when their grandchildren are no longer minors.

At one time, this was the only such building and program in the United States. The concept has expanded so that there are now "grandfamily housing complexes" in at least seventeen American cities. But there is a need for ever so much more.

What can caring grandparents do in support of the housing needs of these grandparents as parents? Very possibly, there are responses on both the macro and the micro level. On the broad scale, individuals and groups can petition city, county, state, and federal housing authorities to facilitate the construction of accessory dwelling units for grandfamilies. On the individual family level, caring friends can be alert, looking for the housing bargains—rental or otherwise—that might come on the housing market. Those who own rental properties can be open to these needs when units become available.[28]

AND SO—

The previous suggestions are not exhaustive and may lead to other possibilities for support. Anne Streaty Wimberly calls upon churches to band together and find ways to offer "intercessory hope" to grandfamilies. They can do so through these and other services and more—so that these families may survive and thrive.[29] Whatever their religious commitment, other grandparents can join the cause.

FOR PERSONAL OR GROUP REFLECTION

1. If you are a grandparent serving as parent to grandchildren, which of the subjects mentioned are most urgent for you? What did the chapter fail to mention?
2. What do you most wish others knew about your experience of being a grandparent as parent?
3. What are the most helpful and hopeful things that have happened in your journey of being a grandparent as parent?
4. If you are a grandparent without parenting responsibilities, do you know any grandparents as parents? What is the nature of your contact with them? What suggestions in this chapter strike you as possibilities for you to be of help?
5. What are your most important takeaways from this chapter?
6. What invitations did you hear in this chapter?

NOTES

1. Deborah Doucette with Jeffrey R. LaCure, *Raising Our Children's Children*, 2nd ed. (Lanham, MD: Taylor Trade Publishing, 2014), 314.

2. Michaeleen Doucleff, *Hunt, Gather, Parent: What Ancient Cultures Can Teach Us about the Lost Art of Raising Happy, Helpful Little Humans* (New York: Avid Reader Press/Simon & Schuster, 2021), 279.

3. Doucleff, *Hunt, Gather, Parent*, 279.

4. Sylvie de Toledo and Deborah Edler Brown, *Grandparents as Parents: A Survival Guide for Raising a Second Family*, 2nd ed. (New York: Guilford Press, 2013), 13.

5. Doucette and LaCure, *Raising Our Children's Children*, 1–9.

6. Andrew Adesman and Christine Adamec, *The Grandfamily Guidebook: Wisdom and Support for Grandparents Raising Grandchildren* (Center City, MN: Hazelden, 2018), 21.

7. National Council on Aging, "Money for Older Adults," accessed November 17, 2019, https://www.ncoa.org/economic-security/money-management/.

8. Doucette and LaCure, *Raising Our Children's Children*, ix.

9. Harriet Hodgson, *So You're Raising Your Grandkids! Tested Tips, Research, and Real-Life Stories to Make Your Life Easier* (WriteLife, 2018), back cover.

10. Kathleen Stassen Berger, *Grandmothering: Building Strong Ties with Every Generation* (Lanham, MD: Rowman & Littlefield, 2019), 66, 67.

11. Kenneth Doka, foreword, in Hodgson, *So You're Raising Your Grandkids!*, xviii.

12. Hodgson, *So You're Raising Your Grandkids!*, 62–63.

13. De Toledo and Edler Brown, *Grandparents as Parents*, 158.

14. This particular list is suggested in Hodgson, *So You're Raising Your Grandkids!*, 63.

15. De Toledo and Edler Brown, *Grandparents as parents* 18.

16. Rae Simons, *Grandparents Raising Kids* (Broomall, PA: Maston Crest, 2010), 11.

17. Stassen Berger, *Grandmothering*, 69. The quotes within her quote are taken from a clinical study reported in the *International Journal of Aging*.

18. Hodgson, *So You're Raising Your Grandkids!*, 32.

19. Hodgson, *So You're Raising Your Grandkids!*, 32.

20. Hodgson, *So You're Raising Your Grandkids!*, 15.

21. De Toledo and Edler Brown, *Grandparents as Parents*, 29–31.

22. De Toledo and Edler Brown, *Grandparents as Parents*, 27.

23. Anne E. Streaty Wimberly, "From Intercessory Hope to Mutual Intercession: Grandparents Raising Grandchildren and the Church's Response," *Family Ministry* 14, no.3 (fall 2000): 22, 23.

24. Doucette and LaCure, *Raising Our Children's Children*, 264.

25. Doucette and LaCure, *Raising Our Children's Children*, 312.

26. De Toledo and Edler Brown, *Grandparents as Parents*, 267.

27. Adesman and Adamec, *The Grandfamily Guidebook*, 66–67.

28. Information on housing and guidance for advocacy came from three sources: Lesley Stahl, *Becoming Grandma: The Joys and Science of the New Grandparenting* (New York: Blue Rider Press, 2016), 97–105; Ronda Kayson, "Multi-Generational Helps 'Grandfamilies' Come Together," AARP, March 6, 2020, accessed December 27, 2021, https://www.aarp.org/home-family/your-home/info-2020/grandfamily -housing.html; and Generations United, *A Place to Call Home: Building Affordable Housing for Grandfamilies*, 2019, accessed December 27, 2021, https://www .grandfamilies.org/Portals/0/Documents/General%20Kinship%20Publications/19 -Grandfamilies-Report-APlacetoCallHome.pdf.

29. Wimberly, "From Intercessory Hope to Mutual Intercession," 35.

Chapter 9

Our Grandchildren's Planet

"We do not inherit the earth from our ancestors; we borrow it from our grandchildren."[1]

"The earth is God's and all that is in it, the world, and those who live in it."

—Psalm 24:1, An Inclusive Version

"In God's hand are the depths of the earth;
The heights of the mountains are God's also.
The sea belongs to God, for God made it,
and God's hands have formed the dry land."

—Psalm 95:4–5, An Inclusive Version

When I asked grandparents, "What concerns you most about this world in which our grandchildren will live?" I heard a variety of responses. Some spoke of how divided and polarized our nation and political leaders are and how paralyzed our government seems to be. Others mentioned violence and the proliferation of gun deaths. Some worried about the increasing distance between the rich and the poor and how hard it is for young people to start a family and buy a home. Others spoke of racial injustice and the disproportionate incarceration of people of color. And there was more.

I hear these grandparents sympathetically, and yet my most basic concern is one that envelops all of these. I am concerned about the hazards of this planet we inhabit—the only one we have. All the other problems exist within this planet, so they must be addressed within this place where we live.

I remember when I first had an inkling of this awareness. When my first grandchildren were born, gradually I sensed that I cared more about the future of this world than I did before they came into my life. Before, I had hoped that at least the world would stay sane and safe to the end of my lifetime and at least a little longer. After they were born, I wanted this safe world for them to the end of their days and beyond.

However, I must confess, I had not yet connected my expanded caring to concrete actions very well. This was in the 1990s, and the community where I lived was beginning a recycling program. Each week as residents put out their garbage barrels, they were also to put another container with the designated items that could be recycled. I was doing this, but—on reflection—not as thoroughly as I might have. During a visit, my daughter Julie observed this and berated me, "Come on, dad. Get with it. That's Daniel and Carolyn's world you're trashing." Thus chastened, I recycled more conscientiously.

Now, thirty-plus years later, those concerns have multiplied into a global crisis. The world's population has expanded to 7 billion people, on its way, some say, to 10 or 11 billion. These people—us—are adding 51 billion tons of greenhouse gases into the atmosphere each year through our living, consuming, traveling, and manufacturing. With the growth of the industrial age, average global temperatures have increased by 1 degree Celsius since the 1850s. If emissions of these gases are not severely reduced, the temperature may increase another 1.5, 2, or even 3 degrees Celsius by the end of the twenty-first century.[2] (One degree Celsius is roughly 2 degrees Fahrenheit.) This, in turn, will produce even more severe weather events such as hurricanes, droughts (with attending wildfires), and raised ocean levels, all of which have been devastating during the year I was writing this book. Life will become even more hazardous, especially for the poor.

Indeed, it is even more dire than that. Bethany Sollereder reports, "The time to prevent climate change, some scientists warn, is past. Now we need to think about adapting, as Earth's climate systems tip out of the stable state they have been in the last 10,000 years."[3]

There are other environmental concerns as well. Huge numbers of species are disappearing—all kinds of plants, insects, birds, and animals. Vast forests are being cut down, waterways are being polluted, and huge collections of plastics float in our oceans.

Pastor and religion and science scholar Ken Whitt concludes, "Our children, grandchildren, and great-grandchildren will experience a world that bears little resemblance to the one they were born into."[4] He takes note of the collapse of systems that sustain human life on our planet, the widespread denial and adaptation by the "principalities and powers of this world," and the fact that much of the damage to the ecosystem cannot be repaired. He concludes that there is no possible return to the "good old days"

A BIBLICAL PERSPECTIVE

Christian believers have a particular perspective for our planet. There is not only our survival, but also responsibility to our Creator. At the very beginning of our Bible, in Genesis 1 and 2, the stories of creation tell us that God created this world out of chaos and pronounced it "good"—six times!—and "very good" one time.[5]

Further, in Genesis 2:15 we are told that God put the persons in this garden of creation "to till it and keep it." Other Bible translations translate this verse "farm and take care of." The word translated as *farm* or *till* (it may be transliterated as *shamar*) is also used in nonagricultural settings, and there the word means "serve, guard, protect, watch over." For example, when in Joshua 24:15, Joshua says, "As for me and my house, we will *serve* the Lord,"—there's that word *shamar* again. Or the blessing in Numbers 6:24–26 begins, "The Lord bless and *protect* [some translations say *keep*] you." The word *protect* or *keep* is that word *shamar* yet again. Fletcher Harper spells out what this means for us Christians as regards our care of the earth. He writes, "We're not here simply to treat the earth as an inert, lifeless, inexhaustible store of resources to use as we please. . . . We're to offer protective service, to work with the Earth in the same kind of caring way that God works with us in our lives."[6]

Scripture further witnesses, time and again, of a world filled with God's creative love. Consider the psalms cited at the beginning of this chapter. Add these words from Psalm 148 (verses 3 and 8–10) in which creation itself is called to praise God:

> Hallelujah! . . .
> Praise God, sun and moon;
> Praise God, all you shining stars! . . .
> fire and hail, snow and frost, stormy wind fulfilling
> God's command!
> Mountains and all hills,
> Fruit trees and all cedars!
> Wild animals and all cattle,
> Creeping things and flying birds!
>
> —An Inclusive Version

This world, created by God and full of God's glory and praise, deserves our tender care! Is This True? Important? Urgent? I am aware that you may disagree with the people I have quoted and with me about the climate. Some don't believe the 97 percent of scientists who agree that this is a crisis. Others say it is hopeless—if for every ton of greenhouse gas we reduce, another country—say China—puts five tons in the atmosphere, why bother? Still others don't believe these temperature changes are caused by humans. They point out that over the long geological story of the earth there have been cold periods and hot periods before—caused by factors other than humans. More recently, there have been several year periods of drought or hurricanes before climate change was being discussed. Of course, scientists have been wrong, and there are other forces at work on our weather and climate.

Still, I feel called to a "grandparent wager." If I am wrong—if there's nothing to this "planet crisis" concern and I have done all I can to avert a crisis that doesn't exist, what have I lost? On the other hand, if I am right, and the impact of this crisis is lessened by the efforts of billions of us, we may have gained a better, safer life for our grand- and great-grandchildren and theirs! That seems to me to be a no-brainer wager. I lose so little if I am wrong and gain so much of what is so important to me if I am right.

Elizabeth Kolbert notes, "In the center of the American Museum of Natural History's Hall of Biodiversity, there's an exhibit embedded in the floor. The exhibit is arranged around a central plaque that notes there have been five major extinction events since complex animals evolved, over five hundred million years ago. According to the plaque, 'Global climate change and other causes, probably including collisions between earth and extraterrestrial objects were responsible for these events.' It goes on to observe, 'Right now we are in the midst of the Sixth Extinction, this time caused solely by humanity's transformation of the ecological landscape.'"[7]

In other words, if a sixth extinction happens, we will have done it to ourselves. That exhibit also includes a quote from Stanford ecologist Paul Ehrlich: "In pushing other species to extinction, humanity is busy sawing off the limb on which it perches."[8]

Whether or not the situation is as dire as I am describing, certainly we are called to a new wisdom about living in this wonderful world, caring for it, and preserving it.

WHAT NOW? HOW SHOULD WE RESPOND?

Out of concern for this planet, which our God created and which our grandchildren have loaned to us for a while, there are three categories of actions we can take. One, there are basic decisions and practices for us grandparents as citizens of this planet. Two, there are subjects to introduce and activities to initiate with our grandchildren. And three, there is a lifetime of practices into which we can guide our grandchildren as they live beyond us (perhaps learning from our mistakes).

Grandparent-Citizen Responses

Live More Simply

Scientist Hope Jahren has been teaching courses on climate change for a number of years. As she has done so, a basic conviction has grown. She recalls, "What was only a faint drumbeat as I began research on this book now rings in my head like a mantra: *Use Less and Share More*." She counsels that while there are ways to conserve energy, "There is no magical technology coming to save us from ourselves. Curbing consumption will be the ultimate trial of the twenty-first century."[9] A place to start is confronting the fact that half or more of the food in the United States is wasted. She asks, "Is this the way we want to live?" Not only waste prevention but also purchasing and using foods grown locally or nearby is wise and useful.

Living simply involves travel as well. Driving electrically powered cars, or eliminating a car entirely in favor of public transportation, walking or biking, and ride sharing are good possibilities. This may also mean less long-distance travel, particularly air travel, which, as Jahren notes "has to be the most resource-intensive way you can spend your day." Her example is being on a plane with two hundred passengers flying from Newark to Minneapolis. She notes that if all two hundred passengers had each individually driven a car for this journey, they would have consumed 40 percent less fuel![10]

If all the fuel and energy in the world were evenly distributed, she notes, the average would be about the same as that consumed per person in Switzerland in the 1960s. She notes that people in that country in those years had a good quality of life. Living more simply did not make them unhappy.

Further, studies have shown that Americans are not happier with their increasing consumption of food and fuel. Indeed, quite the opposite is true. Rather, the Global Happiness Council, exploring happiness in many countries, discovered that six factors figure prominently in people's happiness: social support, freedom to make life choices, generosity, absence of corruption in government, healthy life expectancy, and per capita income.[11] The oldest of us still-living grandparents may know from our earlier lives that people can be happy while living more simply.

Recycle

Another aspect of living simply is recycling. The March 2020 *National Geographic* offered a mind-expanding perspective with a section titled "The End of Trash," with the subtitle question, "Can we save the planet by reusing all the stuff we make?" Author Robert Kunzig begins, "A world without waste sounds impossible. But the vision of a circular economy—where we use resources sparingly and recycle materials endlessly—is inspiring businesses and environmentalists alike. Can we make it happen? Can we afford not to?"

At the beginning of the article, Kunzig offers a picture of a huge trash silo in Copenhagen. It holds twenty-three thousand tons at a time, which is effectively and cleanly burned, generating energy. That is a start, but he notes that "the circular economy aims to end trash by not producing it at all."

He goes on to explore a variety—and combination—of actual experiments in Europe to recycle, refurbish, reuse, and repair. He investigates these strategies at work with metals, machines, energy, clothes, and food. This is based on a circular economy in which a variety of materials and services are recycled time after time. It is an inspiring concept, but even its greatest enthusiasts admit that it is moving too slowly and losing ground to a linear economy with aggressive consumption of more and more goods and services.

Kunzig notes, "Building a circular economy will require an enormous cultural shift, on the scale of the industrial revolution." Its strongest advocates do not think they can do it with the present generation in power; it will take the next generation, and perhaps the next (our grandchildren and great-grandchildren).

In the meantime, what about us older generations? The article has a brief "What You Can Do" box. This is what it says:

- *Restrain yourself.* Fly and drive less. Eat all the food you buy. Wear the clothes you already have. Avoid single-use plastics.
- *Repair and reuse.* Buy fewer, higher quality products and repair them when they break. Donate the clothes you don't wear.
- *Recycle everything.* Compost food waste (or feed it to your pig). Recycle everything you can—and lobby for more recycling.[12]

Invest Sustainably and Justly

For those of us who are fortunate to have retirement accounts that we control or other funds to invest, consider this as another opportunity to care about our planet. There are a number of possible strategies. On the one hand, people can transfer their investments to socially responsible and environmentally friendly industries. A starting place into this is US SIF: The Forum for Sustainable and Responsible Investment.[13] One person selected a social investment option with one of the funds included, and he reports that for a decade, his returns were similar to other modest-risk funds. Another step is to divest from any investments that may have harmful impacts on global warming. Some choose to divest from companies that profit from such activities as mining, drilling, and distributing fossil fuels.

Still another strategy is shareholder activism. Individuals with stocks in a company have the right to vote, to raise questions, and to advocate for environment-friendly strategies.[14] Christopher James, an executive with an investment firm, urges this approach. He writes, "Every investor must vote." His organization succeeded in placing three board members on the ExxonMobil board. These were persons with expertise in transitioning away from fossil fuels, and they had at least some impact on modifying/reducing the corporation's goals for oil production. He points out not only those in investment groups, but individual investors, are part owners and thus have a voice and a vote. He concludes that "investors big and small should make it their goal to vote this proxy season on all environmental, social and governance issues raised at the annual meetings of companies they own. As investors, they have a seat at the table. They should sharpen their elbows and raise their *voices*."[15]

Citizen Initiatives

We have a stake in decisions about our fragile world and we vote in public elections as well! Individual participation and joining with environmental group activities can be an important part of our involvement. Citizen attention and action has drawn response to corroded lead water pipes, poorly placed and smelly landfills, and Native American and other resistance to oil pipelines across rivers and sacred lands. Of course, not all citizen actions are successful. Sometimes the conflict is with powerful and rich forces, and sometimes they prevail. Still, citizen attention and protest has always been part of the way that democratic society functions for the good.

Citizen input is needed to sustain our nation's involvement in the vital global effort to slow or stop climate change. Whether our style is more personal letters to our legislators, supporting major lobbying and environment support organizations, or active demonstrations and protests, our grandchildren's planet hangs in the balance!

In October and November of 2021, the 2021 United Nations Climate Change Conference, also known as COP26, took place in Glasgow, Scotland. While hundreds of governmental and scientific leaders met and thousands more demonstrated and protested outside, negotiation of the steps to prevent catastrophic heating of the planet took place. Some steps were taken, and concessions were made. Still, most assessments see the results as promising very little and that too late. Unless much larger and costly steps are taken, it appears we are headed for climate catastrophe by the end of this century.

Climate activist pioneer Bill McKibben vividly describes "The Basic Math of Climate Change." He points out that scientists tell us that to hold the rise in climate temperature to 1.5 degrees Celsius by the end of the century, we—all the people of the earth—need to cut emissions in half by 2030 and then go on cutting until by 2050 we have completely stopped burning fossil fuels. This first step is possible; "using the brains God gave them, engineers have made incredible progress." Solar and wind power, electric cars, and more can be more widely utilized.

However, McKibben notes, there are also some things we would need not to do: "For instance, we'd have to stop letting our banks and investment managers try to make money off global warming—currently they're . . . investing huge sums in the fossil fuel industry."

And we'd need to share the wealth so that people in poorer parts of the world could have efficient energy such as solar panels as well.

We also need a sense of urgency. The year 2030 is coming fast, probably around 430 weeks from the time this book is published. Climate change, says McKibben, is "a math problem. A hard one, and one that requires we examine our societies and our souls."[16]

Perhaps particularly on this subject, we elders need to listen to young people, including our grandchildren, and their stake in the climate crises facing us. In 2019, *Time* magazine selected Swedish teenager Greta Thunberg as its "Person of the Year." Greta was eight when she heard about the crisis of global warming, but she thought it couldn't be true. If it were, she thought, the politicians would take care of it. When she discovered they weren't, she started her Fridays for Future strikes. At first, this was a lonely protest. Then she was joined by a few others, then dozens, then thousands. On one occasion, she was joined by 7 million young people around the world. Since then, she has been a tireless spokesperson and advocate for the climate.

Thunberg and her following have brought their message to heads of state, to the United Nations, to the pope. As she prepared to ride back across the Atlantic in a sailboat—the least polluting way—she told *Time*, "I'd like to tell my grandchildren that we did everything we could, and we did it for them and for the generations to come."[17] She added, "We can't just continue living as if there was no tomorrow, because there is a tomorrow. That is all we are saying."[18] A teenager challenges us grandparents to ask, can we tell our grandchildren we did everything we could and did it for them?

Practices with our Grandchildren

What, Then, Should We Do?

We have all heard of the concept of the "footprint" including the carbon footprint—the lasting impact some of our activities or actions have had. On the other hand, Jon Biemer introduces us to the idea of the "handprint." A handprint is "a contribution that causes positive change in the world." He adds that this positive change may include "reduction to your own or somebody else's footprint." He points out there is no theoretical limit to what impact a handprint may have, and indeed some handprints can self-propagate.[19]

For example, he suggests a simple and tangible way to have a handprint is to plant a tree. With some care for planting and watering, the tree may grow and provide shade, shelter for birds, erosion control, and perhaps, depending on the type of tree, provide seeds and/or fruits. It will also sequester carbon from the atmosphere. How much? That will vary depending on the type of tree, but one study suggests an average of forty-eight pounds a year, or a ton by the time it is forty years old![20]

Therefore, one of our most important handprints is what we do with our grandchildren to experience nature and the environment, care for it, learn about it, and work to counter the threats to it. Activities we might have done anyway have a new urgency, a handprint for the future.

This begins with inviting and sharing sheer enjoyment, wonder, awe at the world around us. Small children may be interested in so many things—insects, an ant hill, a dandelion about to burst its flying seeds. I remember taking a toddler for a walk in our yard. She was the right height to look down into the blossoming tulips and did indeed look into each one down the row. I had to kneel down and join her—I hadn't seen tulips from that angle before. These explorations might expand to parks, arboretums, zoos, aquariums. Some of these may provide educational experiences that emphasize the need for respect and care for nature as well as doing what we can about the climate.

Further, we can model and teach simple ways to care for this created world. As simple a practice as picking up litter and leaving places neater and more lovely can be a learning experience.

If you are a gardener, teach your grandchildren about gardening. My father was an extensive gardener. When my sister and I were quite young, he helped each of us have a tiny garden with a row of carrots and one of radishes. The first year, I was so eager for a radish or carrot that I had pulled most of them out to see if they were ready far too soon! Thanks to my dad, I am now at least a middling gardener.

Biemer tells that every time his family moved, they repurposed their water hungry lawn. They would "sheet mulch" the lawn with cardboard and wood chips. Then they planted gardens, berry bushes, and fruit trees. In a few years, they were growing enough for themselves and to share with neighbors.[21] Gardens may be large or small. Whatever the size, a garden needs attention from week to week and eventually provides the reward of food we raised ourselves and/or beautiful flowers to enjoy. It also provides an education about the efforts of the food industry and what goes into our having food on the table each day.

Clearly, there needs to be awareness of climate change and all the ways we can reduce our carbon footprint. Conservation practices can be initiated—using less water when brushing our teeth, taking shorter showers, turning out lights when leaving a room, unplugging electronic devices when we are away from home, and adding solar panels for electricity are just a few examples.

In the grade, middle, and high school years, young people will certainly learn about the issues facing our planet. Having candid but calm discussions, taking small but purposeful steps of conservation and doing such practices together are good basic contributions.

Without being alarmist or terrifying children, we need to be clear that this is extremely important and requires all of us to work together so that the climate will not change too drastically. Families of all generations need to learn to work together and influence the wider world toward a just and safe environment.

Reaching beyond Us

Ken Whitt tells of an experience with his four-year-old-grandson, Maxton. He and his wife, Kathy, had taken Maxton and his sister Makenna to the zoo. While visiting various animal exhibits, suddenly the children disappeared. Soon they were located; an animal video had drawn their attention. When it ended, the children (who do not have much screen time at home) were intent on watching it again. The children paid close attention as the film's narrator "painted a stark picture of humanity's cruelty toward animals." Whitt felt sick at this harsh portrayal. He wondered if he should protect them by dragging them away from this disturbing information, graphically portrayed. Before he could figure out what to do, the film ended, and Maxton began passionately to describe in detail what cruel men do to tigers, elephants, and other creatures.

They talked about what they could do about it during their ride home. Weeks later, as Maxton led the prayer at a family dinner, he announced, "When I grow up, I will be a scientist and save the animals." This led Whitt to rethink how to deal with children as regards humanity's abuse of creatures and creation. He concludes, "How much of the darkness from which we adults try to protect our children is exactly the knowledge they must have in order to live and love within the coming perils."[22]

This led Whitt to recall that when Maxton's mother, Lauren, was fourteen, she went with him to Mexico. He led a conference on missions at a Baptist seminary. Then he and Lauren were going to visit some villages, and Lauren was going to help by teaching some children's classes. Early one morning, as they left Mexico City they passed a garbage dump, which by then was home to thousands of people. They saw hundreds of children picking through the garbage, looking for food or anything else salvageable. Lauren later told her father that seeing this heartbreaking sight was life changing. While a life mission had been percolating in her heart, seeing those homeless children led her to know that the purpose of her life would be to provide a loving home to children. Today, she her husband and two birth children are a foster family. Children coming, staying for however long, and going know they are loved out of the life commitment this family has made.[23]

These two stories may point to our next step as regards our grandchildren's planet. This step may be to help these grandchildren become aware of the crisis and challenge of our planet and see what needs to be done. Then we can invite them to discover where their interests, knowledge, and skills might be engaged in responding to this need.

Before concluding this chapter, I need to underscore an important point made earlier. While I stand by all I have said about simple living, ecological handprints, and teaching by example, I also need to acknowledge the greatest problem and most needed action in the climate crisis.

As reported by climate scientist Katherine Hayhoe, the Climate Accountability Institute has concluded that one hundred fossil fuel companies are responsible for emitting 70 percent of the world's heat-trapping gases since 1988!

This is the rapid growth of a long-term problem. Indeed, a 1979 Exxon Petroleum Department report said, "The CO_2 concentration in the atmosphere has increased since the beginning of world industrialization. This increase is due to fossil fuel combustion [and] the present trend . . . will cause drastic environmental effects before the year 2050."[24]

The climate crisis is caused largely by industrial pollution in the last century and a half. It has been steadily increasing and has reached truly crisis proportions. As lovely as all other strategies may be, any hope for our planet involves reducing, restricting, reversing the producing and consuming of fossil fuels as drastically and as quickly as possible.[25] As Hayhoe succinctly summarizes, "It's the system we all live in that must change."[26] Not only the fossil fuel corporations, but we who consume their products need to do that deep change!

THE VOCATION OF CLIMATE CARE

A theme of this book is that grandparenting is a vocation, a call from God about the opportunities and responsibilities that go with this beloved relationship. Furthermore, part of our vocation may be to help our grandchildren to discover theirs! In this chapter, our focus is helping grandchildren discover their vocation to rescue their planet.

Years ago, Frederick Buechner wrote a definition of vocation that struck home and has been widely quoted over the years. Here is part of it:

> There are all different kinds of voices calling you to all different kinds of work, and the problem is to find out which is the voice of God rather than of society, say, or the superego, or self-interest.
>
> By and large a good rule for finding out is this: The kind of work God usually calls you to is the kind of work (a) that you need to do and (b) that the world needs to have done. . . .
>
> The place God calls you to is the place where your deep gladness and the world's deep hunger meet.[27]

Earlier in this chapter, I described the visionary leaders working toward the end of trash and a culture shift, indeed a transformed culture, a circular economy of recycling, conserving, and simpler living. The pioneers in this endeavor anticipated it would take two or three generations to bring it about. Our final step in caring for our grandchildren's planet may be to encourage our grandchildren to discover their part in this brave new and different age. This will be their planet for a while before they pass it on to their grandchildren. May it be at least a fairly safe and abundant space, then and beyond!

FOR PERSONAL AND GROUP REFLECTION

1. What have been your views about planet Earth and its climate? What changes, if any, did you experience in your thinking as you read and pondered this chapter?
2. How are you involved in the various ways mentioned in this chapter as to how people care for our planet? In what ways not mentioned in this chapter? What else might you consider doing?
3. What experiences with nature have you and your grandchildren shared? What other ways can you and your grandchildren learn more and become more involved in creation care?
4. What gifts, abilities, talents, and/or interests does each of your grandchildren have that might serve the earth in making it a safe and good place for all?
5. What are your fears and your hopes as to the future of this planet? For your grandchildren's welfare? What new steps are you willing to take?

NOTES

1. This saying is attributed to many different sources. Some have the word "children" rather than "grandchildren."

2. Bill Gates, *How to Avoid a Climate Disaster* (New York: Knopf, 2021), 3, 24. Gates is in turn summarizing the work of many environmental scientists.

3. Bethany Sollereder, "Climate Change Is Here," *Christian Century* 138, no. 19 (September 22, 2021): 25.

4. Ken Whitt, *God Is Just Love: Building Spiritual Resilience and Sustainable Communities for the Sake of Our Children and Creation* (Canton, MI: Read the Spirit Books, 2021), 136.

5. Genesis 1:4, 10, 12, 18, 21, 25, 31.

6. Fletcher Harper, *Green Faith: Mobilizing God's People to Save the Earth* (Nashville: Abingdon Press, 2015), 33. He is crediting Cal DeWitt for his insight into the meaning of this Hebrew word.

7. Elizabeth Kolbert, *The Sixth Extinction* (New York: Holt, 2014), 266–67.

8. Kolbert, *The Sixth Extinction*, 268.

9. Hope Jahren, *The Story of More: How We Got to Climate Change and Where to Go from Here* (New York: Vintage Books, 2020), 88–89.

10. Jahren, *The Story of More*, 90–91.

11. Jahren, *The Story of More*, 169.

12. Robert Kunzig, "The End of Trash," *National Geographic* (March 2020): 42, 71, 69.

13. US SIF website, https://www.ussif.org/.

14. Jon R. Biemer, *Our Environmental Handprints: Recover the Land, Reverse Global Warming, Reclaim the Future* (Lanham, MD: Rowman & Littlefield, 2021), 35–40.

15. Christopher James, "Every Investor Must Vote," *Time*, January 17/January 24, 2022, 20.

16. Bill McKibben, "The Basic Math of Climate Change," *Sojourners*, March 2021, 18.

17. Edward Felsenthal, "The Choice," *Time*, December 23/December 30, 2019, 48–49.

18. Charlotte Alter, Suyin Haynes, and Justin Worland, "The Conscience," *Time*, December 23/December 30, 2019, 50.

19. Biemer, *Our Environmental Handprints*, 4.

20. Biemer, *Our Environmental Handprints*, 5.

21. Biemer, *Our Environmental Handprints*, 87.

22. Whitt, *God Is Just Love*, 94–96.

23. Whitt, *God Is Just Love*, 96–97.

24. Katharine Hayhoe, *Saving Us: A Climate Scientist's Case for Hope and Healing in a Divided World* (New York: One Signal, 2021), 136–37.

25. Quoted by Hayhoe, *Saving Us*, 137.

26. Hayhoe, *Saving Us*, 150.

27. Frederick Buechner, "Vocation," December 11, 2020, accessed October 2, 2021, https://www.frederickbuechner.com/quote-of-the-day/2020/12/11/vocation.

Chapter 10

Called to Communicate about Our Faith and Values

"I am reminded of your sincere faith, a faith that lived first in your grandmother Lois and your mother Eunice and now, I am sure, lives in you."

—2 Timothy 1:5

"Oh may all who come behind us find us faithful
May the fire of our devotion light their way
May the footprints that we leave
Lead them to believe
And the lives we live inspire them to obey
Oh may all who come behind us find us faithful."

—Jon Mohr[1]

A basic part of our grandparent calling is communicating about what is central in our lives. What and in whom do we believe? How should we live as persons of faith? Where do we belong—what community gives us strength and support and guides us in our serving? And thus, what faith community or communities deserve our loyalty and support? These have never been easy subjects to discuss. Now, in these fast-changing times, they are even less so.

To talk about faith and values, there are three topics we need to consider: (1) where we have been, (2) where we are now, and (3) therefore, what are the ways to carry on these conversations?

WHERE WE HAVE BEEN

I will approach this from the perspective of my own story. I grew up in small-town America. Born in 1934, my childhood and youth years—the

1940s and early 1950s—were in a little community in northwestern South Dakota. My minister father came to a tiny church that had been founded (1911) shortly after the town was (1910), but this church had almost closed during the hard years of drought and the depression.

He brought a loving, caring, servant witness—as did his successor after he died. They consoled the suffering, helped young couples build good marriages, comforted the grieving, were good community citizens, and were there for people in the midst of emergency or crisis. All the time, they gave witness to their faith. People responded, and the church grew. It was down to eight members when we came there, but over the years it grew to more than one hundred. In time there were both whites and Native Americans in the church. When our old building burned in 1949, we all gave and did what we could and sacrificially built a lovely new church.

Not everyone was drawn to our church, of course. There were Methodist, Lutheran, and Catholic churches in town as well. But there was respect and mostly good will among them.

I was baptized, nurtured in my faith in Jesus Christ, and given ways to serve in that little church. It was life changing and enriching for me, and I discerned a call to that ministry. I went to college and seminary in the mid- and late 1950s.

Change in Religious Involvement

In 1960, fresh out of seminary, I arrived at another small town in South Dakota to begin my first pastorate. My intention was to follow the example of my home church and pastors. I would engage in servant ministry, seek the good of the community where I lived, and share my gospel witness. And, I trusted, this little church would become stronger and more vibrant, and lives would be touched there as well.

However, there were two things I did not know. One was that, in 1960, church membership was at an all-time high. In America, church membership had gradually risen from about 45 percent in 1890 to about 60 percent on the eve of World War II (1940). During the war and in the postwar years as GIs returned, married, started their families, church membership soared to around 80 percent in 1960.

Our ministers and home church had done well, but there was also unprecedented openness. Not only our little church but all denominations and religions—liberals and conservatives; Catholics, Protestants, and Jews—experienced this surge in membership and participation.[2]

The second thing I did not know was how abruptly and drastically this was going to change! Sociologists Robert Putnam and David Campbell note that the 1960s were a "perfect storm," powered by many forces at the same time.

They note that there was a shock and two aftershocks that have impacted many institutions, including religious ones to this day.

In the 1960s there was indeed the shock, consisting of many things happening at the same time. There was the huge baby boomer population (including some of the grandparents now reading this!) along with changing sexual mores and morality. Further, there was the vast growth of the use of pot and LSD. In this decade there were the tragic assassinations of both John and Robert Kennedy, Dr. Martin Luther King Jr., and Malcom X. We experienced the polarizing and unpopular war in Vietnam as well as civil rights uprisings and legislation. The Roman Catholic Vatican II Council happened during this time, leading to both affirmation for some and alienation of others among Roman Catholics.

As religious leaders tried to make sense of all this, some wrote about it with the metaphor of the "Death of God." Sales of religious books plummeted by one third during this decade.

All of this had an impact on how people saw religion, faith, religious institutions, and religious leaders. Weekly church attendance nosedived from 49 percent in 1958 to 42 percent in 1969, by far the sharpest decline ever recorded on this measurement.

Even more telling was the change in response to the statement that "the influence of religion in America is growing," an agree/disagree statement included on some polls that were regularly conducted. The percentages of those who agreed with this statement about the growing influence of religion in each year are as follows: 1957, 60 percent; 1964, 45 percent; 1965, 33 percent; 1967, 23 percent; 1968, 18 percent; and 1970, 14 percent. Putnam and Garrett conclude that "almost overnight, it seemed, America had turned from God's country to a godless country."[3]

The political, military, and religious turmoil of the 1960s and the resultant upheaval for all American institutions was the first shock. In the view of Putnam and Campbell, this was followed by two aftershocks.

The first of these aftershocks was the rise of religious conservatism. In the wake of all these events and the moral confusion that came out of them, there was shrinkage in historic protestant churches and a marked growth in conservative churches. People sought guidance, foundation, firm stands on belief and morality. Many found this guidance in the more conservative churches. As part of this, there was an increase in the number of churches that described themselves as "nondenominational."[4]

The second aftershock was the disaffection with religion by many youths and young adults through the 1990s and 2000s. Apparently more and more Americans were unhappy about the large presence of conservative Christian leadership and their support of certain political causes and candidates. This disaffection was strongest among those under the age of thirty.

One clear indication of this second aftershock is the increase of the "nones." They are called this because that is what they check on a religious preference questionnaire. There have always been some "nones," but their numbers have vastly grown. Consider, by their own self-description, "nones" were 5 percent of the population in 1972; 8 percent in 1990; 14 percent in 2000; 18 percent in 2010; and nearly 24 percent in 2018![5] Many more still keep a religious affiliation description but have decreased or ceased their participation in that religion.

Two of the churches I served as pastor have now closed, and the others are much smaller and weaker than years before. My hometown church has merged into a tiny community church with the former Methodist and Lutheran churches. Our lovely building was sold and made into sleeping accommodations, used mostly by hunters during pheasant season.

Values Issues

As part of this seismic shift, a number of morality and value areas underwent change as well. Consider just a few of them.

One was marriage and divorce. In the 1950s and 1960s, divorce was relatively rare. However, in 1969, California passed the first no-fault divorce law, which was later duplicated by most states. While divorce rates rapidly rose and then fluctuated, presently the divorce rate is estimated at about 40 percent. It is likely that many families have had to deal with the realities of divorce and remarriage among some of their family members. There are now more second-marriage families than first-marriage ones.

Another change was the technology and practices of sexuality. The first oral contraceptive pill was approved by the Centers for Disease Control in 1960. This made possible the separation of sexual intercourse from conception and vastly increased the number of people having sex—with or without marriage. For example, one recent study reports that presently 58 percent of high school seniors have had intercourse, but many have avoided pregnancy.

At the same time, there has been much research to benefit those who have not been able to conceive. In vitro fertilization and other methods have sometimes been successful. As has been noted, the various discoveries of the twentieth and twenty-first centuries separated sex from reproduction, and reproduction from sex.

Further, connected to this, there was a vast change with regard to cohabitation, living together before or without marriage. In earlier times, this was frowned upon. If a couple lived together a certain number of years, it was believed they had a common-law marriage. Today such cohabitation is accepted and widespread. According to the Pew Research Center, currently 7 percent of adult Americans are cohabiting, up from 3 percent in 1995. Among adults between the ages of eighteen and forty-four, 59 percent have cohabited at one time.[6]

Yet another value issue that underwent change is response to homosexuality. Through much of American history, homosexuality has been regarded as a personality disorder, a security threat, or a crime. Through the last half of the twentieth and the beginning of the twenty-first century, that view has been slowly changing. For example, in 1973, the American Psychiatric Association removed homosexuality from its list of disorders. In 2015, the United States Supreme Court, in a split vote, ruled that states cannot ban same-sex marriage. Many youths and young adults were far ahead of these agencies in their acceptance and affirmation of homosexuality.

Of course, there are many other values issues that inspire strongly differing opinions—race, guns, prisons, military involvement, abortion, and more. Differing opinions about these and other values are part of the reason for the shrinkage of church participation. As we converse about faith and religion with our grandchildren, these and other values may be part of what we need to discuss.

WHERE WE ARE NOW

We have spoken of the huge growth of the "nones." It is now time to ask, who are they, more precisely? Are our grandchildren among them or influenced by them? Where do various members of our family stand on religious and values topics? What do we need to say to each other and hear from each other? And how do we do so?

The "nones" are a large category, important to understanding the religious landscape. As of the most recent polls, this group is about the same size as both Roman Catholics and evangelical Protestants, the two largest religious groupings in America.

However, "nones"—the religiously unaffiliated—are by no means all alike. Pew Research Center surveys of religious preference provide three categories for the unaffiliated—atheist, agnostic (not knowing), or "nothing in particular." As Ryan Burge notes, "If all the nones were represented by just five people, one of them would be an atheist, one agnostic, and three of them would be nothing in particulars."[7]

It has been long noted that there are at least two ways of engaging religion: believing and belonging. The "nothing in particular" people portion of the disaffiliated, or "nones," do not choose to belong, to be connected to a religious community. However, they may well have religious beliefs, curiosity, and practices.

Philip Jenkins indeed points out that "none" does not equal no religious belief or interest. He notes, "By any reasonable standard, in fact, American 'nones' are a surprisingly religious community. In 2012 a third of the unaffiliated said that religion was very important or somewhat important in their life." He goes on to report that 68 percent of this group of disaffiliated say they believe in God, 58 percent say they often feel a deep connection with nature and the earth, 37 percent classify themselves as "spiritual" but not "religious," and 21 percent say they pray every day.[8]

The "nones" are found in all life stages, genders, and family and economic situations. There is a slightly higher proportion among "nones" of males than females, childless people than those with children, those with higher levels of education than without, and Democrats than Republicans.

One distinction is clear: there are far more among the young than the old—the highest rate of disaffiliation is among the millennials (those born between 1981 and 1996) presently.

Burge notes, "By the time millennials came of age, . . . the wave of secularism was washing across the United States. They walked away from religion in ways that prior generations never considered. I think it's entirely fair to say that Generation X [those born between 1965 and 1981] represents the last generation raised with traditional American religion."[9]

And what about the next generation after the millennials? That would be the group now described as Generation Z, born between 1996 and 2011 or so. In 2021, the Springtide Research Institute released a report on this group. The researchers surveyed a representative group of more than ten thousand persons and conducted in depth interviews with sixty-five persons in this age range. They discovered that the majority of Generation Z consider themselves religious or spiritual, but this does not involve adherence to one specific religion, nor does it likely lead to involvement in one religious group or viewpoint. Involvement in a religious community is even more unlikely.

When Generation Zs were asked what were the most meaningful activities that bring fulfillment to their lives, the top five were: listening to music, spending time with friends, spending time with family, caring for pets, and being outdoors.[10]

When asked who they turned to when overwhelmed and didn't know what to do about something, the top three answers were: my friends, someone from my family, and someone from school. Tied for fourth were "no one" and "someone from my faith community." When the young people were asked, "What were the most useful or important things someone did to help during this challenging time?" the most frequent answers were, "Just let me talk to them," "Helped me see the positive side," and "Helped me identify potential outcomes."[11] Further, 58 percent of the young people told the researchers, "I do not like to be told answers about faith and religions; I'd rather discover my own answers."[12]

This study included a number of quotes from these young people. One of these quotes was about a grandparent. Christopher, age eighteen, commented, "Aside from a couple friends, I have my grandmother, who is very religious. I speak to her about it sometimes, but she has a very old-school mindset to where if I wanted to talk about a topic of LGBTQ+, it would be suppressed very easily and so on and so forth. I don't have a community."[13]

These researchers summarize that what they have found is that many young people do indeed identify as religious or spiritual, and that this contributes to their flourishing. However, they do not accept the whole "bundle" of rituals, practices, and beliefs, of any one church, denomination, or other religious entity.

Rather, they see evidence of "faith unbundled"—"a term that describes the way young people increasingly construct their faith by combining elements such as beliefs, identity, practices, and community from a variety of religious and nonreligious sources, rather than receiving all these things from a single intact system or tradition."[14]

There is another finding from their research that is important for us grandparents to hear. They speak of Generation Z as "America's loneliest generation." They discovered a significant proportion of Generation Z reveal that they are lonely, socially isolated, and stressed. In their survey, more than a third and sometimes almost a half of these young people agreed with the following statements: "I have nobody to talk to," "I feel completely alone," "I feel as if no one understands me," "No one really knows me well," and "It is difficult for me to make friends." The responses were very similar whether the young person attended religious gatherings or not.[15]

Of course, grandparents cannot totally fill the "loneliness gap" that our youth and young adult grandchildren may be experiencing. However, it is good for us to be aware and available.

The grandparents I interviewed probably will not be surprised by what these researchers found and reported about changing religious involvement. I heard several stories of families with generations of membership in the same Christian denomination, but whose grandchildren either refuse confirmation in that denomination, or reluctantly accept it. But then after confirmation, they do not continue to participate in that religion in any way.

WHAT ARE THE WAYS TO HAVE
THESE CONVERSATIONS?

I have painted a picture of vast changes in attitudes and responses to religion, churches, historic faith perspectives, and values practices. These have impacted our grandchildren and us. Now, I hope we discover how to carry on two-way conversations about our faith and our basic beliefs and values. Part of our grandparent calling is to bear witness about what is most important, central, and real in our lives. We are also called to hear from our grandchildren what is important in theirs.

But how do we do this? I will start by sharing a few persons' memories of their grandparents' influence on their life and faith. Then I will suggest some steps and strategies.

Grandparent Faith Stories

Rachel Naomi Remen's Orthodox Jewish Rabbi Grandfather

Rachel Naomi Remen was born prematurely and had a difficult birth. Her parents were told that this meant she would probably be late speaking, if she spoke at all, and possibly experience mental retardation. To everyone's relief, at a Thanksgiving dinner when almost three, she spoke a full sentence: "May I have the salt?"

However her first words were actually taught to her nearly a year earlier by her patient rabbi grandfather, who spent much time with her in her infancy. Her first words were the *Sh'ma* (Deuteronomy 6:4), "Hear, O Israel, the Lord God, the Lord is One," learned in Hebrew. She recalls this was the first of many secrets she shared with her grandpa, and she asked him what the words really meant. He responded, "To me these words have always meant that despite suffering, loss, and disappointment, life can be trusted." He explained he had thought that after all those months in the incubator, her soul had been listening for something to hold on to: "He had hoped that once I found this, I might be ready to begin."[16]

A favorite childhood memory was going to her grandfather's house after school on Friday afternoons, drinking tea with him in his special way—with a sugar cube between the teeth. After they finished, her grandfather would set two candles on the table, light them, and speak with God in Hebrew, sometimes silently sometimes out loud. She would wait patiently "because the best part of the week was coming":

> When Grandpa finished talking to God, he would turn to me and say, "Come, Neshume-le [his favorite term for her, meaning 'beloved little soul']." Then I

would stand in front of him and he would rest his hands lightly on the top of my head. He would begin by thanking God for me and for making him my grandpa. He would specifically mention my struggles during that week and tell God something about me that was true. Each week I would wait to find out what that was. If I had made mistakes during the week, he would mention my honesty in telling the truth. If I had failed, he would appreciate how hard I had tried. If I had taken even a short nap without my nightlight, he would celebrate my bravery in sleeping in the dark. Then he would give me his blessing and ask the long-ago women I knew from his many stories—Sarah, Rachel, Rebekah, and Leah—to watch over me.

She concludes, "These few moments were the only time in my week when I felt completely safe and at rest." In those childhood years, she never felt she was good or smart or disciplined enough to please her perfectionist parents. With her grandpa she felt loved, accepted, and blessed, both by him and by God.[17]

Her parents were socialists and secular. Only once, when she was four, was she allowed to go see her grandpa (an orthodox rabbi and student of Kabbalah, the mystical teachings of Judaism) at his synagogue. The event was Simchas Torah, the day the readings from the Torah are completed and begun again. On this holiday the scrolls are taken from the ark and the men of the congregation dance down the aisles of the synagogue holding the scrolls in their arms. Her grandpa was dancing, holding the largest scroll. When he saw her, he handed the scroll to another man, picked her up and danced down the aisle with her. She recalls, "I remember the little silver bells on the Torah handles ringing and everyone laughing as the men danced all around us with their arms wrapped around the books of wisdom. God seemed very close just then."[18]

Her grandfather died when she was seven. At first, she feared that without him to tell God who she was, she might disappear. But then she realized that she had learned to see herself through her grandpa's eyes, "and that once blessed, we are blessed forever." She closes her book with a blessing to her grandpa, "who knew me before I knew myself and loved me enough to last a lifetime."[19]

Yolanda Pierce's Grandma—and Grandmother Theology

Yolanda Pierce writes of "grandmother theology" and notes that "in a world eager to promote the newest wunderkind, grandmother theology carries us two or more generations back to the kitchens, hair salons, gardens, and church basements of older Black women who are often invisible in theological discourse but without whom the American Christian church would cease to exist."

She adds, "I had a praying grandmother, and nothing I have accomplished would have been possible without her prayers." Not only an ordained minister but a distinguished theological education leader, Pierce recalls the first time she officiated at the communion table. She recalls that when she spoke the words, "For I received from the Lord that which I also delivered to you," she was overwhelmed by the multiple meanings of those words. Among other things it meant that "what I had received, and what this book shares with you are the stories of a faith, birthed in a Brooklyn storefront church and nurtured by the elders who loved me, prayed for me, and set my feet on a solid foundation."[20]

She recalls that when a child "I thought of Jesus as a very close neighbor" and also a friend and confidant. Early in her life she thought that was how everyone believed: "We called on Jesus when the groceries ran low or when someone's fever ran high. We called on Jesus when the rent check was due or when death visited and laid us low. And we called on Jesus in celebration and times of joy—when bodies were healed and prayers were answered and relationships were restored."

Her grandmother rose early in the morning and knelt down beside her bed to pray. Even in her later years, with pain wracking her body, still she knelt. "She sang and prayed, and sometimes she moaned and hummed. But often she just had a conversation with her beloved friend."[21]

Yolanda spent hours over the years of her childhood and youth helping her grandma cook so many things in her spotless kitchen: "Cooking was her ministry and I witnessed as she ministered to the lonely and the sick and the lost with a Bible in one hand and a freshly baked pound cake in the other. . . . She told me that Jesus consistently did three things: healed people, told stories, and fed people. And that is all she, as a follower of Jesus, had to do in order to live a life pleasing to God."[22]

The last night before she left for college, she reluctantly went with her grandma to one more service at the church, a foot-washing service that happened there with fair regularity. She had taken part other times, sometimes washing feet, but never had her feet washed. That night, her grandma guided her where to sit, knelt before her, and washed her feet! At this "my sense of unworthiness brought tears to my eyes, and a spirit of repentance touched the very core of my being." Later the women of the church anointed her forehead with oil in the sign of the cross. In all this they were using simple elements of their faith as they "were preparing to send me away to college and away from their influence. They were calling on God to protect me from the crown of my head to the soles of my feet."

She recalls that while during her senior year of high school, she had attended prom on her first date with a boy, had ridden in a limousine, had traveled outside the country—all for the first time—and graduated first in her class, "those rites of passage pale in comparison to the visceral memory I have of cool water pouring over my bare feet, the feeling of water between my naked unpolished toes, and then the loving hands patting my feet dry."[23]

Cesar Chavez and His Grandmother, Mama Tella

Kat Armas reflects, "Our abuelas [grandmothers] are our connection to our culture, our language, and the country that birthed us. They are our wells of wisdom and memories—both traumatic ones and those necessary for survival. For we who are Latines in the US, our abuelitas hold much of our identities, beliefs, traditions, and theologies."[24]

One example she offers is Mama Tella, whose Catholic faith was deeply influential on Cesar Chavez in the early years of his life. Their family lived far outside the city, and so they were not able to come in to attend the catechism instruction provided there. Nevertheless, the family made the journey into the city one day. They went to the church and asked the priest to give first communion to Cesar and his sister. The priest responded that they could not take communion without taking "formal" religious training. Cesar's mother, Juana, told the priest to ask Cesar and his sister Rita any question from the Catholic catechism to test whether they were ready. Quite to the priest's surprise, they answered every question he asked—Mama Tella had seen to their instruction in the faith. The priest concluded he had no choice but to allow them to receive communion the following day.

As an adult, Chavez led farm workers to organize, work for better conditions and pay, and strike if necessary. He was influenced by Mahatma Gandhi and used nonviolent means, including fasting, to achieve the goals of his movement. Armas concludes, "Chavez, who has been called the Martin Luther King Jr. of the Mexican American community, wouldn't have been who he was without the abuelita theology training he received from Mama Tella."[25]

Russell FourEagles and His Healer Grandmother

Russell FourEagles was born and lived with his parents and siblings in a twelve-by-fourteen tar paper shack in northwestern Wisconsin. When his brother Roy was born, his mother asked the children's grandmother if one of the children could live with her nearby, because there was not enough room for all the children. His grandmother agreed and chose Russell, not yet five years old. She saw gifts in him, partly because at age three he had had a "vision," a prescient dream of his grandfather's death and funeral, though he had never seen one.

He recalls that one day when he was five years old, "Gram" told him that her mother, her grandmother and more than two hundred generations of grandmothers back in time had been healers. And she told him he was to be the next healer. He must learn this so the healing knowledge passed from generation to generation would not be lost. However, to do this, he would have to stay out of the Creator's way. (He would later learn that this meant allowing the power of the Creator to work through him.)

He objected that all those grandmas were women. His grandmother replied there had been some grandfathers as well. She explained that it was okay to be skeptical. The length of time it took him to accept this and understand would be up to him: "The Creator gives us the free will to act or not to act on what he tells us. At first, you, like most people, might not believe; but because you are a healer, you will eventually."

She also told him, "The people who do healing are chosen by the Creator. We are just like a buffalo horn, a hollow vessel to transmit the love [energy] that the Creator sends us."[26]

And so began years with his grandma, as they were together constantly. He spent time with her in the woods and helped her pick the plants and herbs she needed. He learned from her about abundance and treating the earth so that the next seven generations will always have abundance. She taught him the concept of walking the Red Road, which is to walk in a way that honors all creation.

She repeated her lessons for him over and over again. She repeatedly assured him that this was so these teachings from the two hundred generations would not be lost. The practices she taught him had many aspects, but this is one of her core teachings: "First, you have to know that the Creator is going to do the healing. Second, you have to thank the Creator for doing the healing, and you have to do whatever the Creator says. Always keep an intention of healing, and if you *know* the Creator can do instead of just believe he can do, then you are halfway there. The other half comes from our human clients as they practice Oneida breathing."[27]

He has applied his grandmother's teachings in many ways, including aiding his own healing from post-traumatic stress disorder after serving in the military in Vietnam.

And so, after engaging in these healing practices of his culture for more than forty years, he concludes that in honoring his gram's wish that this information not be lost, "I am still running Soaring Eagles Wellness Center and expect to be doing so for some time yet. There are many lessons to teach and teach I will."[28]

Grandparent Strategies for Witness, Learning, and Healing

At the beginning of this conversation in chapter 1 of this book, I noted repeated biblical commands to tell the story of our faith to the generations after us. We are to do this with the assurance that God is faithful to all generations. That foundational Bible teaching guides us as we look for ways to share our faith heritage with the next generations who live in this vastly changed world of religion and values that I have been describing.

How can we be as faithful and transformational as those grandparents I just described? Each of us will have our ways that grow out of our relationships with our grandchildren. Here are some possibilities to consider.

Live and Renew Your Faith. Claim It as the Foundation of Your Life. Live It with Integrity

This may be belaboring the obvious. Still, sociologists of religion have established that "*Parental* [I am adding grandparental] *consistency in word and deed, rules and meaningful intentions* affects the success of religious transmission to children."[29]

Be Faithful, Transparent, and Inviting in Your Faith and Religious Practices and Their Impact on Your Life

One grandpa and grandma told me, "When we visit our children and grandchildren, we enter into how they live their life and do not make demands. If there is no prayer or Sunday worship, we live that schedule with them. When they visit us, we set the atmosphere. They are asked to pause for prayers of thanksgiving at meals, see the devotional materials that guide our quiet times, and come with us to church to worship. There, they will experience our faith community, meet our friends, and discover how our friends know and are interested in them through us." They accept that their grandchildren will find their own way; however, they want them to be aware of the faith heritage of their grandparents.

I heard a similar concern as I interviewed my friend and colleague, Dr. Samuel Park, who at my request had visited with several Korean Christian grandparents, all of whom have lived in the United States for a number of years. He heard them saying that as Christians, they take responsibility for helping their children and grandchildren grow spiritually. They hope their role as Christian grandparents will have the impact that these children and grandchildren will embrace the Christian faith. To this end, they hope to live their lives as a model for their children. They frequently pray for them. One grandmother mentioned that when she sends a birthday card and gift to a grandchild, she always includes a Bible verse. These grandparents he interviewed attend church nearly every week, an example they hope will be followed.[30]

Explore the Possibilities of "Intentional Meals"[31]

Mealtimes provide many opportunities for simple types of faith sharing. Holding hands around the table to express family love and solidarity while thanking God and asking God's blessing on the food and conversation is one way. A simple "table topic," asking each to respond, is another. At a Thanksgiving dinner, for example, the question may be, "What are you most thankful for in the past year?" Your simple response can include a witness you want to share, even as you hear the others. Or another time, "What's the most interesting thing that happened to you since we were last together?" Again, your response can include your faith witness.

There are also the opportunities when a grandparent takes just one grand-child—or perhaps two or three—out to eat at a favorite place. Probably religion will not dominate the conversation, but it might arise as conversation ranges over many things—there may be questions about religious differences, or questions, or doubts, or wonderings.

Engage in Respectful, Mutual Conversation about Faith and Values over the Years—What Has Changed and What Hasn't; What Is Good and What Is Not

Social scientists have also made the commonsense discoveries that family religious conversations are more effective if the elders have warm and affirming relationships with the young, if the conversations are around the questions and topics of concern to the children/young people, and if the quality (acceptance, openness, and warmth) of the conversation is high.[32]

This is important to remember when our conversations with our youth and young adult grandchildren encompass the values and religious changes we have acknowledged in this chapter. For example, a minister-grandpa, a friend of mine, tells me his grandson has rejected his grandfather's faith, seeing it as hypocritical in its treatment of LGBTQ+ people. This friend's denomination was one of the leaders in acceptance of gay people, including authorizing weddings and the ordination of ministers from within the LGBTQ+ community. But it was not soon enough or welcoming enough for this grandson. They will need to live with this difference and still love each other. Each of us may need to hear tough but fair criticism and rejection of some of the things our churches stood for and did in years past. Communication involves both speaking and hearing each other's truth!

There may need to be many frank but respectful conversations about our beliefs and practices with regard to sexuality, cohabitation, and recreational drugs—but not only personal morality topics. There may also need to be conversations about Black Lives Matter, climate change, right-left politics (sometimes tougher topics than religious differences!), and more.

And perhaps you will need to talk about whether "organized religion"—and the beliefs and teachings of the church of which you have been a part—have anything to offer your grandchildren, or it they will need to find another way for their spiritual journey.

Invite a Grandchild to Join You in Any Possible Service or Mission of Your Faith in Which You Are Involved

Perhaps shared involvement in some action will speak louder than words. If you help out at a food kitchen, or serve meals at a homeless center, or deliver for Meals on Wheels, ask a grandchild to go along and help you. If you march or demonstrate for a cause connected to your faith and values, invite support and presence from the children and young people in your family. Serving, rather than talking, may be where you are closer to each other.

Sensitively Communicate What You Believe and Whom You Trust

Even amid all the changes we have been describing, there may be a time to make sure it is known what you believe and why. I have treasured the guidance of 1 Peter 3:15, particularly in the language of the King James Version: "Be ready always to give an answer to every [person] that asketh you a reason of the hope that is in you with meekness and fear"—or, as the NRSV translates it, "with gentleness and reverence." Times may have changed, but you are called to speak of the faith, commitments, values that have guided you and the God who has sustained you.

Recognize How Essential Family, Including Grandparent, Conversations about Faith and Values Are

Again, I turn to the social scientists who note that religion in America has changed "from being in essence a communal solidarity project to instead being a personal identity accessory." In other words, religion has changed from something the community supports into a personal/individual exploration. This, they say, parallels "the transformation of family from being institutional to companionate to individualistic."[33]

A consequence is that, in large part, families no longer depend on their faith communities to communicate religious belief, doctrine, and practice to their young; the families do it themselves. Grandparents are part of those families and may have important gifts to offer—the gifts of lived experience and long perspective.

Respect Family Boundaries

In all this, there is an important caution: Good grandparenting is always supportive of and respectful of the children's parents. We do not contradict, undermine, or second-guess our grandchildren's parents. There may be delicate times when we need to be, believe, and behave as who we are, but at the same time, we should not intervene in the family life and practice of our children and grandchildren.

Pray and Trust!

An important thing that grandparents can do is pray—faithful daily prayer for each family member by name—prayer for their safety, their welfare, and their spiritual journeys. These prayers may also include thanksgiving for each family member, for each individual's unique personality and gifts, and for what they mean to the grandparent.

Another important thing we can do is trust. This is a word I need for myself. As I mentioned at the beginning of this chapter, I have spent my life trying to help the church be a faithful, broad-visioned, and compassionate presence in the world. I hoped the church would be stronger at the end of my ministry than it was when I began. It saddens me that the church as I know it is much weaker, its future and viability under question.

I need to learn to trust that again God has more light and truth to break forth. Further I need to believe that there will be a different but new church, or something like it, that it will have its form, witness, and contribution to that different age. Perhaps my grandchildren or theirs will be part of it.

FOR PERSONAL AND GROUP REFLECTION

1. How does your experience compare to mine as to what has happened to the church and religious participation?
2. How do you feel about your interactions about your faith and commitments with your grandchildren? What has been your most rewarding experience? Your most frustrating? What is missing that you would like to add to family faith conversations?
3. What from your life and faith do you most want to pass on to your grandchildren? What do they have to offer you?

4. What causes or issues, important to you, do you hope family members will continue to support after you are gone?
5. What is your deepest hope as to the faith and practice of your grandchildren?

NOTES

1. Jon Mohr, "Find Us Faithful" (courtsey of Birdwing Music and Jonathan Mark Music, admin. by Capitol CMG Publishing, 1987).

2. Robert Putnam and Shaylyn Romney Garrett, *The Upswing: How America Came Together a Century Ago and How We Can Do It Again* (New York: Simon and Schuster, 2020), 133–34.

3. Putnam and Garrett, *The Upswing*, 138.

4. Robert D. Putnam and David E. Campbell, *American Grace: How Religion Divides and Unites Us* (New York: Simon and Schuster, 2010), 100–20.

5. Linda Mercadante, *Belief without Borders: Inside the Minds of the Spiritual but Not Religious* (New York: Oxford University Press, 2014), 2; Ryan P. Burge, *The Nones: Where They Came From, Who They Are, and Where They Are Going* (Minneapolis: Fortress Press, 2021), 28.

6. Juliana Menasce Horowitz, Nikki Graf, and Gretchen Livingston, "The Landscape of Marriage and Cohabitation in the U.S.," Pew Research Center, November 6, 2019, accessed November 9, 2021, https://www.pewresearch.org/social-trends/2019/11/06/the-landscape-of-marriage-and-cohabitation-in-the-u-s/.

7. Burge, *The Nones*, 101.

8. Philip Jenkins, "Is American Christianity Really in Free Fall?" *Patheos*, October 22, 2019, https://www.patheos.com/blogs/anxiousbench/2019/10/is-american-christianity-really-in-free-fall/.

9. Ryan Burge, "'OK Millennial': Don't Blame the Boomers for Decline of Religion in America," Religion News Service, August 30, 2021, accessed September 29, 2021, https://religionnews.com/2021/08/30/ok-millennial-dont-blame-the-boomers-for-decline-of-religion-in-america/.

10. Springtide Research Institute, *The State of Religion and Young People: Navigating Uncertainty* (Farmington, MN: Springtide Research Institute, 2021), 60.

11. Springtide Research Institute, *The State of Religion & Young People*, 43.

12. Springtide Research Institute, *The State of Religion and Young People*, 68.

13. Springtide Research Institute, *The State of Religion and Young People*, 51.

14. Springtide Research Institute, *The State of Religion and Young People*, 59.

15. Springtide Research Institute, *Belonging: Reconnecting America's Loneliest Generation* (Farmington, MN: Springtide Research Institute, 2020).

16. Rachel Naomi Remen, *My Grandfather's Blessings: Stories of Strength, Refuge, and Belonging* (Thorndike, Maine: G.K. Hall, 2001), 220–22.

17. Remen, *My Grandfather's Blessings*, 35–36.

18. Remen, *My Grandfather's Blessings*, 437–38.

19. Remen, *My Grandfather's Blessings*, 37, 460.

20. Yolanda Pierce, *In My Grandmother's House: Black Women, Faith, and the Stories We Inherit* (Minneapolis: Broadleaf Press, 2021), xviii–xix.

21. Pierce, *In My Grandmother's House*, 5.

22. Pierce, *In My Grandmother's House*, 34–37.

23. Pierce, *In My Grandmother's House*, 132–35.

24. Kat Armas, *Abuelita Faith: What Women on the Margins Teach Us about Wisdom, Persistence, and Strength* (Grand Rapids, MI: Brazos Press, 2021), 28–29.

25. Armas, *Abuelita Faith*, 29.

26. Russell FourEagles, *The Making of a Healer: Teachings of My Oneida Grandmother* (Wheaton, IL: Quest Books, 2014), 14.

27. FourEagles, *The Making of a Healer*, 49.

28. FourEagles, *The Making of a Healer*, 240.

29. Christian Smith and Amy Adamczyk, *Handing Down the Faith: How Parents Pass Their Religion on to the Next Generation* (New York: Oxford University Press, 2021), 6.

30. Samuel Park, Zoom conversation with the author, October 8, 2021.

31. Josh Mulvihill, *Biblical Grandparenting: Exploring God's Design for Disciple-Making and Passing Faith to Future Generations* (Minneapolis: Bethany House, 2018), 158.

32. Smith and Adamczyk, *Handing Down the Faith*, 5–6.

33. Smith and Adamczyk, *Handing Down the Faith*, 91.

Chapter 11

Leaving a Legacy

"Set up waymarks for yourself, make yourself guideposts; consider well
the highway, the road by which you went."

—Jeremiah 31:21 (RSV)

"A child who has a grandparent has a
softened view of life, the feeling that
there is more to life than what we see,
more than getting and gaining, winning and losing.
There is a love that makes no demands."

—Lois Wyse[1]

What legacy or legacies would you like to leave your grandchildren? The
dictionary definitions of the word *legacy* are rather straightforward. For
example, according to Merriam-Webster, a legacy is:

1. something (such as property or money) that is received from someone . . .
2. something that happened in the past or that comes from someone
   in the past.
3. something that happened in the past or that comes from someone in
   the past.[2]

However, if we apply the term *legacy* to grandparents and grandchildren, it
becomes rich and nuanced. It offers a new dimension of our Christian calling
as grandparents, for we consider not only what immediate impact our grandparenting offers but also our long-term influence. This includes the continuing influence, individual and collective, we hope to have even after we die.

I have been reflecting on this for quite some time, and I also asked a couple
dozen grandparents "What legacy/legacies would you like to give to your
grandchildren?" Their answers were varied and fascinating. I will summarize

their answers and my experiences as I reflect about the legacies we receive and those we provide.

OBJECTS

One of my granddaughters would like my coffee cup when I am gone, and I will be glad for her to have it. It is a sturdy cup in various shades of blue. Originally it had the name "Dick" on it in black, but the dishwasher gradually erased that away years ago.

I don't know why she wants it, but I imagine it is because from the time she was born, every time they visited us, I would be drinking from it at breakfast or break times. I think she may have her other grandpa's cup as well. For whatever reason, she is welcome to it.

The objects we leave may have intrinsic value; that is to say that the item would have some monetary or aesthetic worth whether the person receiving it had any attachment to the original owner or not. Or an object may simply have extrinsic value—whatever significance it has arises from the love, emotions, sentiments that exist(ed) between the giver and the receiver.

For example, over the years, my mother was given Black Hills gold rings—these had monetary value, to be sure, but also were especially loved by folks with roots in South Dakota. When she died, she still had three of those rings and had requested they be given to her three granddaughters—my children. Those were legacies with both intrinsic and extrinsic worth to them. Other intrinsic legacy gifts might include not only jewelry but China, antiques, a prized piece of furniture, or a much-loved vehicle—anything that would be considered valuable to an uninvolved person.

And there are many legacy items that are strictly extrinsic. For example, the only things I have that were my dad's are two notebooks of his sermon outlines/notes and his Norwegian Bible. Once in a while, I take out one of those notebooks and read through a few of those sermon outlines. I can still see him, sitting at his ancient upright typewriter, typing fairly quickly using just one finger from each hand, the result rather faint, as he did not change the ribbon very often. On the corners of the pages are penciled in when and where (and how many times) he preached it in those groups of small churches he served.

I followed in his footsteps into ministry, but it was years after he died. So we never had a chance to "talk shop" or reflect together on our calling. These notebooks are as close as it gets for me, and so I treasure them.

Grief therapists speak of "linking objects." Harriet Hodgson writes, "Linking objects—things that belonged to a deceased loved one—are reminders of experiences and feelings. A bereaved son may wear his father's watch, for example, and a bereaved daughter may use her mother's dishes. At holiday time I put mother's cut glass water decanter on the dinner table, a reminder of her love, guidance, and all the wonderful meals she made. Objects like these are sources of comfort. . . . This connection can last for months or years."[2]

I think those notebooks are linking objects for me. With regard to the notebooks, I was amused when, after having them for decades, I looked a little more carefully at the items in a pocket in the back of one of them. I found several unused penny postcards and also a number of unused three-cent stamps—from the 1940s. Some value I did not know I had! I don't know what they are worth—intrinsically—and am in no hurry to find out.

A person's artistry or skillfulness may have produced items that were intended for immediate use and enjoyment, but which endured and became legacies. I think of a beautiful corner cupboard Mary Ann's dad made for her mother many years ago to match a new dining room set they had purchased. It is still a treasure in our home. I also think of the afghans and tablecloths her grandma crocheted. Or I think of the quilts Mary Ann has made for family members' births, graduations, and marriages, and also the delightful and original Christmas stockings she made for each new member who joined our family by marriage or by birth. Each of these is enjoyed, stirs memories of the loved one who created it, and will continue to do so after that person is gone.

The grandparents with whom I visited sometimes noted a playful aspect to objects that might be part of their legacy. Kathleen kept diaries of the times she and the family with her granddaughters went on Disney cruises and other enjoyable times. These will be left to her granddaughters to recall those golden days. Ron M. has designated in his will that his sons receive the baseball glove he made when he was younger. "It is a real piece of junk," he said. "It will give them something to argue about—like who gets it throw it away"—a memento of his adventurous spirit and things he tried, not always successfully.

ITEMS THAT PORTRAY FAMILY HISTORY

Chapter 4 discussed possible family roles for grandparents, including that of a griot, storyteller, and historian to tell the family about their roots and heritage. Some grandparents do this not only verbally but with created materials. These also may be legacies. Rosemary has created three family photograph albums, one for each of her children's families. She has also written a least a hundred pages about their family story and will also give a copy of that to each of her children's families.

Lois Wyse tells of a great-grandmother who had been diagnosed with incurable cancer and was in hospice care. One day, when her daughter made a supportive phone call to her—a call she expected to be difficult—she was surprised by her mother's upbeat tone.

Her daughter asked her what happened, and she replied she had a project. Someone had given her a book for a grandmother to fill in. She explained, "There are pages to write about my parents and childhood, about you and all the children, grandchildren, and great-grandchildren in our family, and I cannot tell you what joy it gives me to relive the best—and sometimes the worst—of everything I have known."

The daughter was glad but still amazed at how contented she sound.

Her grandmother replied, "I am taking time to know where the sweet and the bitter are to be found, and I am putting it all on paper. This is a very exciting thing for me to do because the very act of re-creating my life fills me with life. And because I am doing this, I know that I will not die. Every time you open this book, I will come alive. That's quite a wonderful thing for a great-grandmother to realize."[3]

This has been something I also have done and am doing. Even as I work on this book, Mary Ann and I are creating a little book of stories from our childhood for our great-grandchildren, so they will know who we were, who our parents were, and also how crazy we were about them when they came, a new generation in our family story.

REAL ESTATE AND FINANCES

When I ask about legacy, I sometimes hear a story that goes something like this: "When we were a young couple, we bought a lot on a lake we enjoyed. At first, we would just camp out there, then we built a little shack. Over the years we built a more comfortable summer home, and as the family grew, added bedrooms. Our family has had so many good times there. We will leave it to our family members with the hopes that it will be a source of family enjoyment for many years to come." They speak of the legacy of families enjoying being together and the place where it often happened. And they are privileged enough to own it and to be able to give it away at the end of their lives.

Others answer my question with a financial response. Doug and Frieda probably spoke for many grandparents when they replied, "We hope to have a little money to share with them."

Some grandparents will have a lot of money to give, and some very little. Grandparent love cannot be measured by how much there is (or whether there is any) in the bank at the end of life's experiences, illnesses, and challenges. Large or small, the spirit of giving continues to the end of our days.

This again stirs a memory. When my mother died, she had made known that she had several certificates of deposit in a local bank. As these came due, she directed that half of them were for my sister, Ruth, and half were for me. The total came to a few thousand dollars for each of us.

Neither of us needed that money for any survival or emergency needs. Still, it touched us deeply that to the end of her days, Mom wanted to have something to give us! And we hoped she had not deprived herself of anything she needed in order to do so. She had done enough of that earlier in our lives together.

Those who expect to die with larger assets have probably sought legal advice about the prudent way to give it so that the resources are given as they intend, to those whom they want to receive them, with the fewest encumbrances.

Our decisions about what to do with our resources when we die constitute a legacy, not only in what we give our family members but in what we give elsewhere. A will can also be a witness to one's faith and life priorities. If one has been a tither to God's work and to specific churches, ministries, schools, or other agencies of mercy, a tithe or more of one's last resources to those entities may do some good and give survivors a witness.

Ruth Westheimer and Steven Kaplan remind us, "A final bequest to your own favorite cause is also a fitting statement about your life and your wishes."[4]

RESCUED, PRESERVED, AND GUIDED LIVES

For some grandparents, their legacy will be the people who needed and received their care.

In chapter 8, I wrote of grandparents who, usually out of crisis or tragedy, needed to become parent to their children's children. Anne Streaty Wimberly reports the reflection of one such widowed grandfather. When his son-in-law committed suicide and his daughter "just fell apart" in the aftermath, he took their children, both boys, into his home. Thus began a life of many responsibilities and activities.

He recounts, "There's cooking and making sure they have clean clothes . . . trip after trip to the school to make sure they do what they're supposed to do . . . homework I don't understand. I mean for them to go to college. God knows they are smart enough. . . . I follow them around to their sports activities and take them to the doctor. We go to church together, and they are in the youth group. I like to think that I'm passing along to them what they need to make it in the world. . . . If I just succeed in setting them in the right direction in life, then I'll have accomplished something important!"

Indeed! Wimberly notes that grandparent-parenting "holds within it a special opportunity to leave a legacy."[5] Certainly, this tired but happy and involved grandpa will have no trouble identifying what his legacy is!

Others may leave a legacy in the friendship, encouragement, support they offer another. I think of my home pastor, who was like a second mother to me, and also a counselor, mentor, encourager, and guide in my life and work. When she died, I needed to grieve and talk about her, so I called my friend Ron E.

Ron listened to me for a while, and then he responded, "Dick, she left a lot of gifts, and you are one of them." He was right. I am part of her legacy. There are many others.

A KINDER, SAFER WORLD

Some grandparents responded to my question about legacy with hopes for a turnaround on difficult societal issues, for a better world for their grandchildren to live in. As noted in chapter 9, many of us grandparents view the planet, its pollution, and its changing climate with alarm and fervently hope to influence the vast changes that must be made. We want so deeply for our grandchildren to live on a safe, inhabitable planet.

Amy voiced hope for another change: "My grandchildren are so precious. However, in the view of the world, they are not precious. I want them treated fairly, with equal opportunity. I also hope that the grinding poverty that makes it hard for so many children and families to succeed can be addressed."

There have been many who have left some legacy seeking a better and safer world for us who come after. In this connection, I was interested to learn of the origin of Mother's Day. Anna Jarvis started a campaign for a Mother's Day in 1905, the year her mother Ann Reeves Jarvis died. She wanted a day to remember her mother and her campaign for the end of war and killing.

A Wikipedia article notes, "Ann Reeves Jarvis had been a peace activist who cared for wounded soldiers on both sides of the American Civil War, and created Mother's Day Work Clubs to address public health issues. She and another peace activist and suffragette Julia Ward Howe had been urging for the creation of a 'Mother's Day for Peace' where mothers would ask that their husbands and sons would no longer be killed in wars."[6]

Anna Jarvis later objected to all the commercialism that became associated with the day she had labored to create. We will honor this legacy when we again make the holiday the "Mother's Day for Peace" and observe it by not sending their husbands, children, and grandchildren to war where they may be killed.

A similarly spirited contemporary group is the Raging Grannies. Founded in Canada, they have used their humor, old-fashioned granny costumes, and songs (paraphrases of old-time melodies) to make cogent comments and protests on social concerns. There are now also many groups in the United States. On their website, they introduce themselves with these words:

> We are totally non-violent, believe in only peaceful protest (with lots of laughter), work for the "many not the few" . . . and see our work as the spreading green branches of a great tree, rising up to provide shelter and nourishment for those who will come after us.

> Grannies are best equipped to make public, corrupt things that have been hidden (often for profit). Local toxic waste sites that no-one seems prepared to tackle, asbestos sites employing young people desperate for work, nuclear waste products being dumped outside an uninformed small town, laws that affect an entire community, passed quickly with no opportunity for study. The list goes on.[7]

Questions, protests, humor, imaginings of another and a better way to a better world are among the legacies grannies and gramps can have.

VALUES AND EXAMPLES TO BE FOLLOWED

Other grandparents answered my question about legacy with the most basic advice they would offer a grandchild, a statement of one or a group of principles or something they hoped they modeled for their grandchildren.

For example:

Carl W.: Find something that can be a lifetime job that will earn you a living and learn to do it well.

Bob: Love and care about other people. Do what you can to make others' lives better without any defining rules and regulations.

Carl and Mary Ann R.: Do good. Love and be kind to one another. Live by the Golden Rule and Micah 6:8. I [Mary Ann] have sung anthems about these all my life. I would like my grandchildren to live by these truths.

Ron and Carol S.: We want them to develop their own faith and have confidence in themselves. We want them to have compassion for everybody, not just the people they know and love. There is always something you can do for someone.

Jeanie S.: In my life, I played a leadership role. I was mayor of a small city and led in establishing the first comprehensive recycling program in the state. I want them to know women can be leaders and that they should take care of the earth.

Kathy: Try to live by the greatest command to love God and treat neighbor as selves. Live by Matthew 25—feed people, take care of people. Stand up for what is right. That's pro-life.

Archie: Value education, a good work ethic, a deeply held faith.

In this chapter I have spoken of several aspects of what I hope my legacy to be. I also hope my legacy will include the example of dying peacefully, with trust and with gratitude for having been allowed to live long enough to know each of my grandchildren and great-grandchildren. My last prayer each night is Jesus's prayer on the cross: "Father, into your hands I commit my spirit" (Luke 23:46). I hope to die with that prayer on my lips, and that my grandchildren know of my peace and trust in living and dying.

PLAYFULNESS, HUMOR, LIGHTNESS

Some of the responses included hopes for humor and laughter as they are remembered.

Alan expressed his legacy hopes for his grandchildren in this way: "First to have a sense of humor; second care about their neighbors, particularly those who have less than you do. Be engaged in whatever you do in life—I don't care what you do but do it well. These are the guideposts I hope for them. Remember grandpa and have a good laugh."

Ron M. similarly noted, "I am interested in a lot of stuff, some of which I do well. Others I just fiddle at until I quit it. I want them to feel free to laugh at me after I die."

I also hope my grandchildren will laugh and smile at memories of me. I hope they remember how delighted I was in them, how much fun we had together, and how many games I let them win.

LOVE AND RELATIONSHIPS

Some answered the question about legacy by speaking of the relationship they wanted their grandchildren to remember.

Lois: How much I loved them; remember that and give that love to the next generation. I have always wanted to be the best example I could of what they could be in the next chapter of their lives. Family is so important. Family to me is everything.

Ron and Carol S.: We want them always to know we loved them and support them, and that we will continue to do that even after we die.

Terry, a smitten, relatively new grandpa: "If my grandchildren say, 'Baba loved me.'"

AND SO—

For many of us, the question about what legacy we want to leave stirs a prior question: What legacies did we receive? Ann reflected, "What is the legacy of my grandparents? I have memories. My grandmother lived what she believed, and she loved me."

I find myself recalling the words we recite at communion services "For I received from the Lord what I also handed on to you" (1 Cor. 11:23). We received God's blessings and guidance from those who went before us, and we are now the temporary stewards of those gifts to hand on to those who come after us.

Such thinking is deep and solemn. It may make us uncomfortable to consider. But it is necessary, and it is inescapable. This is where our calling as grandparents has been leading from the day that each of them was born. Certainly, it deserves the best of what has been given to us, the finest that is within us, and our intention that our legacies be named and given.

FOR PERSONAL AND GROUP REFLECTION

1. What is the most basic legacy you have received from those who went before you?
2. Do you have objects that were given to you, a legacy from someone who cared about you?
3. Do you own objects that you intend to give to some family member as part of your legacy to them? Have you made those intentions known in some way—spoken or in writing?
4. Do you have plans and guidance for passing whatever of finances or property to the persons or causes you choose? What steps have you taken that this happen? What questions or unresolved issues do you have about this?
5. What church, school, cause, or organization might you like to give a gift as part of your legacy?
6. What beliefs, commitments, or values would you like to pass on as part of your legacy?
7. What, if any, laughter or play, do you think there is in your legacy (or that you want to be in your legacy)?
8. What love and relationships do you want affirmed in your legacy?

NOTES

1. Lois Wyse, *Grandchildren Are So Much Fun, I Should Have Had Them First* (New York: Crown Trade Paperbacks, 1992), 94.

2. Harriet Hodgson, "Grief's Linking Objects: The Winnowing Process," Open to Hope, November 12, 2016, accessed November 22, 2021, https://www.opentohope .com/griefs-linking-objects-winnowing-process/.

3. Loise Wyse, *You Wouldn't Believe What My Grandchild Did . . .* (Thorndike, ME: Thorndike Press, 1994), 96–98.

4. Ruth Westheimer and Steven Kaplan, *Grandparenthood* (New York: Rutledge, 1998), 227.

5. Anne E. Streaty Wimberly, "From Intercessory Hope to Mutual Intercession: Grandparents Raising Grandchildren and the Church's Response," *Family Ministry* 14, no. 3 (fall 2000): 27–28.

6. "Mother's Day," *Wikipedia*, accessed January 21, 2022, https://en.wikipedia.org /wiki/Mother%27s_Day.

7. Raging Grannies International website, accessed January 21, 2022, https:// raginggrannies.org/.

Chapter 12

Surprised by Joy and Spiritual Growth on the Grandparent Journey

"O Lord, my heart is not lifted up, my eyes are not raised too high; I do not occupy myself with things too great and too marvelous for me. But I have calmed and quieted my soul, like a weaned child with its mother; my soul is like the weaned child that is with me."

—Psalm 131:1–2

"Becoming a grandparent is a miracle, an affirmation from God.
Having grandchildren makes you want to embody
those spiritual qualities of love and forgiveness.
It makes you feel like a spiritual role model; it keeps you on your toes.
It warms your heart!"

—Kathleen

Some years ago, I was pastor of a church with a number of young families in it. From time to time, when planning for the next Sunday service, I would say to my associate, Dick Fears, "Next Sunday we are dedicating some babies." (Baptists have this service, similar to the baptism of infants in other denominations.) "No," Dick would gently correct me, "next Sunday we are going to dedicate some *parents and* babies." He was right, of course. From my perspective now, he would have been even more correct if he'd said, "grandparents, parents, and babies." Indeed, sometimes grandparents came and stood with their children and grandchild as they made promises and bowed in prayers of thanksgiving and trust for this child. Generations offered themselves in rededication in response to being entrusted with this new child in their midst.

JOY AND GROWTH WITH THE
ARRIVAL OF THE GRANDCHILD

One of the forms of that child dedication service begins, "Every child comes into the world with the message that God is not discouraged with the world, for God continues to create." Indeed, one source of joy and spiritual growth on this grandparent journey is the very arrival of the child, for each child is a gift, a trust, a source of awe and joy, an invitation to grow spiritually. As noted in chapter 2, this is true whether the child arrives by birth, by adoption, or by the family growing and reconfiguring with a remarriage.

An essay I read recently expresses this truth beautifully. In "Four Things My Newborn Taught Me about God," M. P. Antoine reflects that he professionally works with older children. When he and his partner were expecting a child, while he hoped for a healthy infant, he expected to wait till the child grew for bonding moments. However, he writes, "Imagine my surprise when . . . God treated me to theology lessons courtesy of a seven-pound squirmy potato." Four theology lessons, actually.

The first is that all humans carry within them a spark of divinity. He recalls, "I held him in my arms less than a minute after his birth, and the feeling I got when his eyes met mine—vibrant, alert, and most of all alive—was nothing less than an encounter with the divine." The second is that breath is the spirit in motion. In this regard, he recalls that the Hebrew word *Ruach* can be variously translated as breath, wind, spirit of humanity or spirit of God. "That moment, hearing the first breath of life where previously there was none, was an encounter with the Holy Spirit." This in turn helps him be more aware of the spirit at work in all sorts of other places and times.

Third, he discovered that joy is a renewable resource. As they share the news, photos, Zoom conversations with physically distant and sometimes estranged family, "my son's birth has been a way to mend bonds between estranged people, to share in the joy that accompanies a new life." And fourth, not everything must be said to be heard. Though Antoine confesses he is a "words person," he admits, "I've had to learn how to rely less on words and more on presence. Instead of telling I can show love, letting my actions speak for me . . . I can even lend him some of my peace." This in turn reminds him of the sheltering love of God, recalling Jesus' desire to gather people together "as a hen gathers her brood under her wings" (Matt. 23:37).[1]

This father is learning and growing spiritually as he responds with open heart to his infant son. I would love to read his developing thoughts and experiences in the years ahead!

His reflections take me back to the birth of my first child. I also had virtually no previous experience around infants. Like him, I was blown away with wonder. I was in my final year of theological school and had many assignments to complete as well as a little church to serve. However, nothing seemed so important as to be home near our baby, perhaps holding, rocking, feeding, or changing her; perhaps just sitting by the bassinet looking at her.

I was taking a course in group therapy at the time. The professor, who knew Mary Ann, wrote her a congratulatory note. He also told her that group therapy was wasted on me. All I did was sit in a corner of the classroom and look contented!

My life was richer; I had more to live for. I was growing spiritually.

A similar but somewhat different spiritual growth spurt came nearly twenty-five years later when that firstborn child gave birth to her firstborn—our first grandchild. This birth expanded my vision and led me to think of my family extending and surviving after I have left the earth.

There was a sense of second chances and new beginnings. Many have spoken of hoping to be better grandparents than they were parents. I felt—or at least I hoped—that when I was with this grandchild (and the others when they came), I would not also be worried about all the other responsibilities to which I needed to attend. I would have time for them.

This was an escape from the midlife blahs. Here was a new person to love unconditionally, to imagine possibilities and a future for, to pine for when separated, to brighten my thoughts and my days. And to think (as I said in the introduction) how I resisted and dreaded becoming a grandpa!

In chapter 2 I also mentioned Lesley Stahl's exhilaration and ecstasy at the birth and at being in the presence of her granddaughter. She learned of the brain pathways of baby love, and of feeling the bonding hormone oxytocin when near the child. I find it reasonable to believe that this organic, visceral response is a gift to us from beyond ourselves, from the divine.

Stahl describes the experience from a female perspective. I don't know how much this varies from grandmothers to grandfathers. Certainly, gender aside, people experience becoming grandparents in different ways. Not everyone is as ecstatic. Still, even for those whose response is more muted, welcoming a grandchild is an occasion for wonder and for growth.

In a playful reflection, Stahl comments, "Children are the dessert course of life, or as Steve Leber who founded Grandparents.com told me, 'God gave us grandchildren to make up for aging.'"[2] At very least, many older adults are much happier than society in general imagines, and a big source of this happiness is our grandchildren.

Betty Shannon Cloyd recalls William Wordsworth's saying that children come from heaven, "trailing clouds of glory." She finds herself reflecting on that when in the presence of a newborn. She tells of a granddaughter recently born into their family. One day her husband was carrying this child, "this tiny pink bundle of love," and asked her, "Since you have just come from heaven, do you have a fresh word from God for us?" When Betty asked him what her reply was, he answered, "Chloe said, 'I am the fresh word from God!'"

She reflects, "Babies are indeed a 'fresh word to us from God' and by their very being speak to us of all that is pure and innocent and holy."[3]

JOY AND GROWING INTO A SPIRITUALLY RESOURCEFUL PERSON

So far we have spoken of the spiritual growth that comes from the arrival and presence of grandchildren among us. But there is more. We live out our lives together and want to model, witness, and teach what is true about God and life and faith. When we begin this part of the grandparent journey, a further spiritual growth opportunity happens.

For example, Jeanie comments, "Becoming a grandma has deepened my spiritual life, because I want to be a good example for them. It has made me think more about who I am and helped me want to grow spiritually." Part of her commitment is expressed in leading a women's group discussing books on spirituality and prayer.

Joan recalls the blending of spirituality and music in the faith journey of her family and how thrilling it is for her to hear her granddaughter play "The Lord's Prayer" so beautifully on her violin.

Doug and Frieda S. reflect, "Being grandparents has made us more aware of how important our values and beliefs are. Things matter because of what we leave behind." They look within to find a delicate balance between sharing their lively involvement in church and progressive political causes with respecting different points of view and less involvement of other members of their family.

In chapter 10, I wrote of communicating faith and values to our grandchildren. In this chapter, we look at this from the other end—how it enriches us as we try to be the person worthy and able to teach these things.

Again, Shannon Cloyd has a wise word for us, pointing to what she believes is the most necessary component for being this kind of guide. "It is this: To be a spiritual guide for our children we have to be on the journey ourselves." Further, she says, quoting her spiritual mentors, "the effective spiritual guide is 'one who knows that his or her first duty is to see to his (her) own interior life . . . since you will never be able to give to others what you do not possess yourself.'"[4]

Shannon Cloyd goes on to suggest that out of the richness of tending to one's own spiritual journey, there may be a variety of gifts/roles the caring adult can offer a child. Her list includes these: (1) Holy listeners, (2) amateurs who reflect God's love, (3) friends of the soul, (4) those who point beyond themselves to the kingdom, (5) companions in the difficulties and joys of life, (6) God's ushers, and (7) gate openers for the spirit.[5]

Her emphasis, like mine in chapter 10, is on what to offer and how to influence the child/grandchild. I mention her possibilities to suggest how enriching it can be for a grandparent to aspire and live a life from which to carry on these conversations.

Trying to be worthy spiritual companions to our grandchildren may take us on a daunting journey of self-examination, self-correction, improvement, and growth. We grandparents are of many different personality types and will thus experience and express our spiritual relationship with God and others in different ways. And so, different ones of us will respond, or not, to various of the possibilities I am about to mention. That's fine! I invite honest self-examination and developing your spiritual life in grandparenting in a way that fits you.

For starters, think about language. Many an adult has had the experience of a small child hearing an inadvertent slang or curse word and repeating it—sometimes at a most inopportune time! None of us are perfect, but is our speech—not only with regard to cursing, but also respect for family, opponents, ethnic groups, and more—the speech we would hope our grandchildren would emulate?

Or what about compassion and generosity? Have you become jaded about the many appeals, or do you feel pain when catastrophes happen or someone is hurting? Are you one of those who show up with tools or a hot dish when someone has had trouble?

And what about relationships with members of your family? With those who serve you in public? With persons who disagree with you politically, or persons of other races or ethnic groups? Are you open, respectful, and caring/relationship building when it is hard to do so?

How does your spirituality relate to creation, the wonder and beauty of nature, the gift of gardening, and pleasure in and concern for the world around us?

What about worship and participation in your faith community, taking part in mission, learning, or growth opportunities there? Remember that a predictor of whether male children will continue in public worship is whether the adult males in their life do so.

And what about prayer in your home, prayers at mealtimes, quiet time, meditation, and regular reading of scripture and other sacred literature? What feeds your soul and renews you? Do you regularly engage in the spiritual practices that have the potential to renew you?

Specific religious and spiritual conversations or participation in worship times may be a very small part of what you do with grandchildren. However, I contend that everything else you do or experience with your grandchild is also a spiritual relationship with that grandchild. My former colleague Maynard Hatch, at the time professor of Christian education at the seminary where I taught, used to say, "You cannot not teach Christian education." The implication was that you would either do it consistently—matching words with action and being—or you would do it inconsistently. That calls for our growth as persons.

Physician Rachel Naomi Remen recalls such an invitation to growth while attending a physicians' seminar on listening. This happened when, as guided to do so, they all took out their stethoscopes and listened to their own hearts for several minutes. Eventually, after their earlier anxiety at this exercise, they heard the steady, reliable beat on which their lives depended. She recalls, "It was a profound and ineffable encounter with the mysterious"—the "sort of moment my grandfather [an orthodox rabbi] would have blessed."

After a time of silence, one of the cardiologists spoke about his work, seeing it as something holy. Then he said aloud a prayer that he had heard some time back:

> Days pass and the years vanish and we walk sightless among miracles. Lord, fill our eyes with seeing and our moments with knowing. Let there be moments when your Presence, like lightning, illumines the darkness in which we walk. Help us to see, wherever we gaze, that the bush burns, unconsumed. And we, clay touched by God, will reach out for holiness and claim in wonder, "How filled with awe is this place and we did not know it."[6]

That prayer embraces the openness and reach for becoming that kind of grandparent who will be a faithful and reliable mentor, witness, guide on our grandchildren's spiritual journeys.

JOY AND GROWTH THROUGH A FAITH COMMUNITY'S ACCEPTANCE

So far, I have spoken of two aspects of spiritual growth in grandparenting: the joy of becoming grandparent and the call to grow into a faithful and consistent spiritual mentor with one's grandchildren. As I visited with grandparents, I heard another story—one other way.

Carol S. told of her experience with her first grandchild: "When Autumn was born, my son—her father—was going through one of his rough patches. Holding this child was healing for me. Maybe I couldn't care for my son right then, but I could care for his daughter. Her parents were not married. We did not hide that at church. I can't imagine taking a child that was born out of wedlock to church, but that is what we did. If they hadn't accepted our granddaughter, we would not still be at that church. But there was just no questions asked. She was a child of God and loved by God. She was loved and welcomed from the first day."

This little girl is now twelve and about to enter the youth group of that church. Her grandmother reached out to her church for support, perhaps testing to see if they were what they said they were for her in her time of pain. She and her granddaughter received what they so deeply needed. Now she offers grandmother care and wisdom throughout the ministries of that church.

AND SO—

I proposed this book to my editor and then undertook to write it out of the wonder and awe that grandparenting brought into my life. This was true not only in my life, but in our marriage. One of the strengths of our marriage had been parenting together. It was also true of our grandparenting. We each brought our gifts and interests to our grandchildren and supplemented the care we provided when they were entrusted to us. They in turn enriched our marriage.

Grandparenting became the focus of our scheduling. What grandchild event, recital, play, concert, or sports event did we need to plan as to arrivals and departures? How could we be part of as much as possible, encouraging, supporting, and affirming? Though we never lived in the same community as our grandchildren, we traveled many miles to spend those times together. It was good when their parents made equal efforts in our direction.

Until a grandchild arrived, I had no idea how spiritually enriching and enlightening that arrival would be. However, on a shelf in my study, there is a reminder of my beginning to discover this. It is a picture of this first six-week-old grandson and me—I am holding him, still in my clergy robe, as I greeted worshippers after the morning service. He leans into and rests on my shoulder. I am filled with delight to introduce him to my faith community, and my faith community to him. His trust and my unhidden delight in having him close can be plainly seen.

Much as I loved that moment, I was only beginning to see all of what this calling into grandparenthood entailed. I was called into a broader vision, a wider fellowship, and a deeper and wider-ranging commitment than I had first realized. I have loved that journey of discovery and will continue to do so as long as God gives me breath.

However, at age eighty-eight, I realize my journey on this earth won't go that much longer. I celebrate each day, each time I get to be with a grandchild or a great. And I think of them and pray for them every day.

Wherever you are in your grandparent journey, God's rich blessings to you and yours as you grow into all that I have described in this book and more! Grace and peace. Amen.

FOR PERSONAL AND GROUP REFLECTION

1. What are your stories of entering grandparenthood? How do they compare to mine?
2. What comes to mind as you think about the spiritual dimension of being grandparent?
3. On pages 155–156, I suggest a variety of areas for possible new disciplines and growth as a grandparent. Which are you doing well? What beckoned to you from those suggestions?
4. What do your grandchildren have to teach you spiritually?
5. I have contended that grandparenthood makes old age happier and more joyous. Is that your experience as well? If so, in what ways has grandparenthood increased your happiness?
6. What are your intended next steps of growth as a grandparent—spiritually and in other dimensions?

NOTES

1. M. P. Antoine, "Four Things My Newborn Taught Me about God," *Patheos*, December 7, 2021, accessed December 9, 2021, https://www.patheos.com/blogs/christiansingeneral/2021/12/four-things-my-newborn-taught-me-about-god/.

2. Lesley Stahl, *Becoming Grandma: The Joys and Science of the New Grandparenting* (New York: Blue Rider Press 2016), 257.

3. Betty Shannon Cloyd, *Parents and Grandparents as Spiritual Guides: Nurturing Children of the Promise* (Nashville: Upper Room Books, 2000), 32.

4. Shannon Cloyd, *Parents and Grandparents as Spiritual Guides*, 39. In the quote within this quote, she is citing Tilden Edwards, who is in turn quoting Thomas Merton.

5. Shannon Cloyd, *Parents and Grandparents as Spiritual Guides*, 53–54. Each of these is elaborated in her following pages.

6. Rachel Naomi Remen, *My Grandfather's Blessings: Stories of Strength, Refuge, and Belonging* (Thorndike, ME: G.K. Hall, 2001), 95.

Postscript

The Grandparent Vocation in Our Declining Years

"I believe that I shall see the goodness of the LORD
in the land of the living.
Wait for the LORD;
be strong and let your heart take courage;
wait for the LORD!"

—Psalm 27:13–14

"For the most part, grandparents are not about power, fame, money, or sex, but rather about love—perhaps the purest and least exploitable love—that humans can feel for one another."

—Mary Pipher[1]

On a recent visit to my grandson and his family, I was delighted when my two-and-a-half-year-old great-grandson came to the table where the adults were visiting over their coffee, took me by the hand—chose me!—and led me to his play area. With a bit of caution, I got down on the floor with him and entered his little tent in the corner of the room. We played back and forth with his push toys, and we looked together at the books he wanted to show me. I let him play with my phone for a little while, something he loves to do. As with other times together, he checked my gold-colored wristwatch, hoping, that like other people's watches, it would do more than just tell time. These one-on-one moments with this special child were what I most hoped for in the visit. I was so happy!

After a while, his interest was wandering to some of the other guests, and the floor was getting hard. So he went to interact with them. His watchful daddy, my grandson, came, offered a hand, and helped me up on my feet and into a comfortable chair.

LIFE AND GRANDPARENTING
CHANGES WITH THE YEARS

This experience is a vignette of where I am now and what is coming in my grandparent journey. Of course, I still deeply love each grandchild and great-grandchild, but there is much I cannot do with or for them anymore. I cannot pick up and carry around even a twenty- or thirty-pound child, and I cannot care for a child on my own for an afternoon or a day. I do not drive anymore and so cannot take them on a special outing or shop for a special gift. Other grandparents will have other things they can no longer do—for example, cook, bake, or entertain and house grandchildren as they once did.

I am looking at this from the early part of the old-old stage of the older adult life journey. Other changes are happening, and more are coming. Even with hearing aids, I sometimes do not hear or understand what is said. Sometimes when I want to speak, it takes a while to remember or express my thoughts. Words come slowly, and too often, someone jumps in and tries to speak for me. Each change impacts my grandparent-grandchild experiences.

In this season of life, health and vigor go only one way—they decline. My mobility and balance probably won't stay as good as they are. The possibility of dementia increases vastly as we age, and it can take many different forms.

The time may come when I can no longer leave my apartment, or perhaps even my hospital bed. My days are numbered. I am not being morbid; the God who has guided and sustained me thus far will continue to be with me. Hopefully, my journey to the end of life will be peaceful, with a minimum of pain, and I will die quietly with prayers of trust on my lips.

GRANDPARENT LOVE LIVING WITH LIMITATIONS

How do we live our sacred vocation of grandparenting in our final years? Grandparents have been called "the giving-est of all people." What do we do when we can no longer give—or at least not give in the same way? Here is a list of possibilities.

Receiving Care as Giving

To begin, we may need to discover that receiving care should not be a sign of shame or defeat. Rather, we can learn that receiving can be a form of giving. Jesus received the woman's costly perfume, Zacchaeus's hospitality, his followers' support and prayers.

It is true that as we learn to receive, we may also need to learn a happy balance. Some of us hate to ask for anything, even when we really need it. Others of us tend to demand more than what others may want to give. It's good to seek a middle way. Then, with our caregivers and especially with our grandchildren, we may discover the "holiness of receiving."[2]

Some of the grandparents with whom I visited were experiencing this already. Joan has visits from her two young adult grandchildren. They live some hours away but come as frequently as possible. She recalls a recent visit with her grandson: "Mormor (a Norwegian word for grandmother)," he asked, "What's it like? Are you okay living here by yourself? Are you lonely?" She treasures those visits and feels their care deeply.

Kathy has had recent surgery and numerous doctor visits. She relates, "In our family, whoever needs help asks; whoever has it is there to provide it. I am already in that phase now. I am getting help with all my transportation needs willingly from my grandchildren."

Terry, now a grandfather himself, recalls hours of sitting with his parents-in-law during their closing years and months of frailty that included dementia: "It was a privilege to be there, to give them something to drink, to be with them at the end of their lives." He adds, "They accepted this with graciousness."

A granddaughter recalls, "My grandmother had always insisted on cooking for us. It was such a gift when she allowed me to bring lunch to her and my grandfather."

Loving Attention

Grandparents speak to me of giving loving attention by learning how to negotiate the various electronic ways their younger generations communicate. They follow their grandchildren on Facebook and other media platforms, enjoy the pictures they send on phones or other devices, telephone each other, and send and receive texts. They learn to talk and see each other on FaceTime or perhaps gather with the family on one of those group platforms.

What is so natural to younger people takes time, intentionality, and effort for older adults. This is especially so as sight and hearing deteriorate. Further, computers, phones, and social media devices sometimes need someone to straighten out our confusion and our messes!

"All Will Be Well"

Kathleen responds, "When my granddaughters came to visit me at the retirement community, they loved sitting by the glowing fireplace or walking down the spiral staircase. 'You live in a beautiful place, Grandma,' they told me.

I hope to go on living here, enjoying their visits. I hope to continue to show an interest in their lives. As best I can, through the rest of my years, I will continue to model for them that growing old is okay."

Setting Limits, Finding Renewal

Further, we recall that Jesus took time to rest and pray, to set boundaries around his time and energies. In like manner, we will be wise to learn how lovingly to state the boundaries of our limited strength and energy. We can be clear about what activities are helpful or not and possible or not, and if possible, how long and how extensively should we take part. For many of us older people, routines are part of what holds life together and helps us do as well as we are doing. It is a kindness to others and to ourselves to be clear about this. That way we may find ways both to be available to family and live within what is possible.

Part of Jesus's boundaries involved taking time for rest and prayer, renewal, and guidance. This can be our practice as well. Our needed quiet times can include loving prayer. We can hold up each family member—child, grandchild, great-grandchild, in personal and frequent prayer—an intangible but real gift for each of them.

Loving through the Veil of Dementia

Part of our aging journey may include some form and degree of dementia, memory loss, forgetfulness, or confusion. If so, I hope for us the sweet spirit of one woman. Her granddaughter told me that as she sat with her grandmother, Grandma would smile at her and say, "You know, I can't remember who you are, but I'm sure I love you."

Lynn Casteel Harper recalls her grandfather's relationship with her as he lived with dementia. Earlier in his life, she wrote that her grandfather "had enjoyed center stage, relished the spotlight." He had been a military pilot, a popular physician, a Rotary International ambassador, a public speaker, a jazz trombonist, and a gifted vocal soloist and song leader. She recalls, "I admired my grandfather but did not feel close to him."

She continues,

Years later, in my grandfather's late dementia, I experienced a new tenderness in him, as the spotlights darkened and the houselights softly came up. He was no longer on stage. He was in a wheelchair. He lived in a nursing home where no one knew him from any other old veteran. He did not speak much. He hummed on occasion. . . . A new stillness eclipsed his earlier frenetic disposition. At first, it was hard to receive this new faintness as a gift. . . . But once I adjusted to the lower light, I felt a kind of exhalation: relief. For the first time in my life, I saw with my grandfather, eye to eye, no showing, no telling, no clapping. While his past light had beamed, attracting my attention and admiration but rarely my affection, his new darkling light was inviting, even gentle.[3]

Amazingly, the trajectory of their relationship was not one of loss and greater distance because of his dementia, but of drawing closer together in vulnerability, mutuality, friendship. As she later reflected, "My relationship with my grandfather in his later years was no 'horror story' . . . as a certain calm connection grew between us."[4]

Their story contains hope and invitation—perhaps if/when dementia comes, there can be a quiet time of mutual love and care, not of deterioration of the love that exists between us and our grandchildren.

End of Life Clarity

As we live out our years, another gift we can give family is clarity about our end-of-life wishes. When our life is fading, what treatments do we want, and what do we not want? This can be done either informally or more formally though such documents as a living will, advance directive, or health treatment directive.[5] Harper recalls that her grandmother was very clear about her end-of-life wishes, which was such a gift to the family. When she suffered a sudden and massive brain bleed, her daughter—Lynn's mother—knew she would not want risky surgery nor an extended but lesser quality of life. "Because of my grandmother's clarity and her communication of her wishes to our family, my mother had great peace about her decision to decline the surgical option and seek comfort care for her mother."[6]

Guidance for When Life Ends

It can also be a gift to family members to communicate about your wishes for after you die. What worship, remembrance, or ceremonies would you like? Are there scripture, readings, songs you would like included in a celebration of your life? Would you like to write (or have you written) your own obituary, and if so, where is it? What would you like to be done with your body? Where should your remains be placed? Are there particulars that people should know that will make it easier for them as they grieve your death?

Of course, these questions may be painful and uncomfortable. Still, you can show love to your family by helping them go through this chapter of your family's life. It will help them do this with grace and strength if they know your wishes in this regard.

Legacies Revisited

Chapter 11 explored the subject of legacies, including objects that might have intrinsic or extrinsic value, larger gifts and bequests, values guidance, and enduring relationships. As life draws near to a close it is good to do what is possible to see that your legacy intentions are fulfilled, and that gifts and reflections will be shared with their intended receivers. It may be important or necessary to restate your legacy wishes and intentions. Legacies point beyond us and leave evidence of our life, witness, and caring with those we love who will endure after us.

In our final frail years, the content and ways we give may change. The love behind those gifts will not.

FOR PERSONAL AND GROUP REFLECTION

1. How long have you been a grandparent? How has grandparenting changed for you over those years? How has it stayed the same? What further changes do you anticipate?
2. If you have parents or grandparents who died, what did they do well in communicating their care and intentions in the final years of their lives? What, if anything, was left undone or unsaid? Where you would have liked a further word?
3. What felt most important to you in this chapter? What did it miss or leave out?
4. What do you aspire to as regards your final frail years and your grandchildren?

NOTES

1. Mary Pipher, *Another Country: Navigating the Emotional Terrain of Our Elders* (New York: Riverhead Books, 1999), 275–76.
2. In this and many parts of this section of the chapter I am summarizing and paraphrasing a generous, detailed letter of January 29, 2022, that Lynn Casteel Harper wrote in answer to my request for her personal and professional perspective on this topic.
3. Lynn Casteel Harper, *On Vanishing: Mortality, Dementia, and What It Means to Disappear* (New York: Catapult, 2020), 127–28.
4. Harper, *On Vanishing*, 175.
5. A workbook with these documents is available at https://www.practicalbioethics .org/resources/caring-conversations/.
6. Harper, letter to the author.

Appendix A

The Twenty Questions

In chapter 4, we noted how having a "strong intergenerational self"—knowing one's family's story and heritage helps contribute to a child's well-being and ability to cope. These questions contribute to that intergenerational self. These come from the research of Marshall Duke and Robyn Fivush of Emory University and are included with Duke's permission. Talk about them and enjoy them with your grandchildren.

TWENTY QUESTIONS

Please answer the following questions by circling "Y" for "yes" or "N" for "no." Even if you know the information we are asking about, you don't need to write it down. We just wish to know if you know the information.

1. Do you know how your parents met? Y N
2. Do you know where your mother grew up? Y N
3. Do you know where your father grew up? Y N
4. Do you know where some of your grandparents grew up? Y N
5. Do you know where some of your grandparents met? Y N
6. Do you know where your parents were married? Y N
7. Do you know what went on when you were being born? Y N
8. Do you know the source of your name? Y N
9. Do you know some things about what happened when your brothers or sisters were being born? Y N
10. Do you know which person in your family you look most like? Y N
11. Do you know which person in the family you act most like? Y N
12. Do you know some of the illnesses and injuries that your parents experienced when they were younger? Y N
13. Do you know some of the lessons your parents learned from good or bad experiences? Y N

14. Do you know some things that happened to your mom or dad when they were in school? Y N
15. Do you know the national background of your family (such as English, German, Russian, etc.)? Y N
16. Do you know some of the jobs your parents had when they were young? Y N
17. Do you know some awards that your parents received when they were young? Y N
18. Do you know the names of the schools that your mom went to? Y N
19. Do you know the names of the schools that your dad went to? Y N
20. Do you know about a relative whose face "froze" in a grumpy position because he or she did not smile enough? Y N

Important Note: About that last question—15 percent of our sample actually answered "yes"! This is because the stories that families tell are not always "true." More often than not they are told in order to teach a lesson or help with a physical or emotional hurt. As such, they may be modified as needed. The accuracy of the stories is not really critical. In fact, there are often disagreements among family members about what really happened! These disagreements then become part of the family narrative. Not to worry![1]

NOTE

1. This is quoted from Marshall P. Duke, "The Stories That Bind Us: What Are the Twenty Questions?" *Huffington Post*, May 23, 2013, accessed February 9, 2021, https://www.huffpost.com/entry/the-stories-that-bind-us-_b_2918975. The questions are included here with his permission.

Appendix B

Websites That May Be of Interest

Raging Grannies International, https://raginggrannies.org/
Their site opens with these words, *"Please, pour yourself a cup of tea and join us inside.* . . . We are out in the streets promoting peace, justice, social and economic equality through song and humour. If you want to join us, please read through our site then contact us."

The Long Distance Grandparent, www.thelongdistancegrandparent.com
Kerry Byrne sends out a free monthly newsletter with ideas and suggestions for rich long distance grandparenting. She also offers "The Long Distance Grandparent Society," for a subscription cost. This provides a "Monthly Connection Pack," a "Monthly Connection Chat," expert interviews, workshops, and a members-only Facebook group.

Grand: Living the Ageless Life, https://www.grandmagazine.com/
At this site, one can register for the free online *Grand* magazine, which includes articles across a wide range of grandparent-grandchild topics. This is a service of the pioneering Grandparenting Foundation, founded and led by Dr. Arthur Kornhaber.

Legacy Coalition, https://legacycoalition.com
The Legacy Coalition is a Christian organization that offers a wide range of books and other resources and an annual conference to help grandparents learn and grow in their faith impact on their grandchildren.

Raising Grandchildren,https://www.aarp.org/relationships/friends -family/info-08-2011/grandfamilies-guide-support.html
The AARP provides this basic beginning resource for grandparents serving as parents.

The Cool Grandpa: Living, Learning, Loving, http://cool-grandpa.us/
Greg Payne became a grandpa at age forty-eight and didn't feel he knew much about it. So he created a website with podcasts and other resources to create a supportive community of learning for grandpas.

Bibliography

AARP. "2018 Grandparents Today National Survey." Accessed September 15, 2021. https://www.aarp.org/content/dam/aarp/research/surveys_statistics/life -leisure/2019/aarp-grandparenting-study.doi.10.26419-2Fres.00289.001.pdf.

Addiction Center. "Facts and Statistics of College Drug Abuse." Accessed October 26, 2021. https://www.addictioncenter.com/college/facts-statistics-college-drug -abuse/.

Addyman, Caspar. "Why Babies Laugh." TED Talk. November 29, 2017. https://www.youtube.com/watch?v=mymMye4purU.

Adesman, Andrew and Christine Ademec. *The Grandfamily Guidebook: Wisdom and Support for Grandparents Raising Grandchildren.* Center City, MN: Hazelden, 2018.

Alter, Charlotte, Suyin Haynes, and Justin Worland. "The Conscience." *Time,* December 23/December 30, 2019.

Antoine, M.P. "Four Things My Newborn Taught Me About God." *Patheos,* December 7, 2021. Accessed December 9, 2021. https: //www.patheos.com/blogs/ christiansingeneral/2021/12/four-things-my-newborn-taught-me-about-god/? utm_ source=Newsletter&utm_medium=email&utm_campaign=Best+of+Patheos&utm _content=57&lctg=32930.

Armas, Kat. *Abuelita Faith: What Women on the Margins Teach Us about Wisdom, Persistence, and Strength.* Grand Rapids, MI: Brazos Press, 2021.

Baker, Beth. *With a Little Help from Our Friends: Creating Community as We Grow Older.* Nashville: Vanderbilt University Press, 2014.

Bates, James S., and Alan C. Taylor. "Grandfather Involvement and Aging Men's Mental Health." *American Journal of Men's Health* 6, no. 3 (2012): 229–39.

Biemer, Jon R. *Our Environmental Handprints: Recover the Land, Reverse Global Warming, Reclaim the Future.* Lanham, MD: Rowman & Littlefield, 2021.

Bonczar, Thomas P. and Allen J. Beck, "Lifetime Likelihood of Going to State or Federal Prison." Bureau of Justice Statistics, March 1997. Accessed October 26, 2021. https://bjs.ojp.gov/content/pub/pdf/Llgsfp.pdf.

Bonner, Timothy. "What Has Happened to Christianity in the US?" Good Faith Media, October 21, 2021. Accessed October 21, 2021. https://goodfaithmedia.org/ what-has-happened-to-christianity-in-the-u-s.

Borgman, Lori. *What Happens at Grandma's Stays at Grandma's.* Eugene, OR: Harvest House, 2021.

Buechner, Frederick. "Vocation." December 11, 2020. Accessed October 2, 2021. https://www.frederickbuechner.com/quote-of-the-day/2020/12/11/vocation.

Burge, Ryan P. *The Nones: Where They Came From, Who They Are, and Where They Are Going.* Minneapolis: Fortress Press, 2021.

———. "'OK Millennial': Don't Blame the Boomers for Decline of Religion in America." Religion News Service, August 30, 2021. Accessed September 29, 2021. https://religionnews.com/2021/08/30/ok-millennial-dont-blame-the-boomers-for-decline-of-religion-in-america/.

Calkins, Raymond. "Exposition of II Kings," *The Interpreter's Bible*, Volume 3. New York: Abingdon Press, 1954.

Campbell, D. Ross. *How to Really Love Your Grandchild . . . in an Ever-Changing World.* Ventura, CA: Regal, 2008.

CDC. "Increase in Developmental Disability among Children in the United States." Accessed October 25, 2021. https://www.cdc.gov/ncbddd/developmentaldisabilities/features/increase-in-developmental-disabilities.html.

De Toledo, Sylvie and Deborah Edler Brown. *Grandparents as Parents: A Survival Guide for Raising a Second Family.* Second Edition. New York: Guilford Press, 2013.

"Dixon Chibanda." *Wikipedia.* Accessed November 2, 2021. https://de.wikipedia.org/wiki/Dixon_Chibanda.

"Dixon Chibanda—The Friendship Bench." Hearts on Fire. Accessed November 2, 2021. https://www.heartsonfire.org/dixon-chibanda.

Doucette, Deborah with Jeffrey R. LaCure. *Raising Our Children's Children: Room in the Heart.* Second Edition. Lanham: Taylor Trade Publishing, 2014.

Doucleff, Michaeleen. *Hunt, Gather, Parent: What Ancient Cultures Can Teach Us about the Lost Art of Raising Happy, Helpful Little Humans.* New York: Avid Reader Press/Simon & Schuster, 2021.

Duke, Marshall P. "The Stories That Bind Us: What Are the Twenty Questions?" *Huffington Post*, March 23, 2013. Accessed February 9, 2021. https://www.huffpost.com/entry/the-stories-that-bind-us-_b_2918975.

Egan, M. Winston, and Linda Egan. *Grandparenting on Purpose: Fresh Ideas, Activities, and Traditions for Connecting with Grandchildren Near and Far.* Millcreek, UT: Winnprint, 2020.

Erdrich, Louise. "We Live in a Haunted Age" (Interview by Hugh Delehanty). *AARP Bulletin*, November 2021.

Erikson, Erik H. *Childhood and Society.* Second Edition, Revised and Enlarged. New York: Norton, 1963.

Eyre, Richard. *Being a Proactive Grandfather: How to Make a Difference.* New York: Familius, 2017.

Feiler, Bruce. *The Secrets of Happy Families.* New York: William Morrow, 2013.

———. "The Stories That Bind Us." *New York Times*, March 17, 2013. Accessed February 9, 2021. https://www.nytimes.com/2013/03/17/fashion/the-family-stories-that-bind-us-this-life.html.

Felsenthal, Edward. "The Choice." *Time*, December 23/December 30, 2019.

FourEagles, Russell. *The Making of a Healer: Teachings of My Oneida Grandmother.* Wheaton, IL: Quest Books, 2014.

Fowler, Larry. *Overcoming Grandparenting Barriers: How to Navigate Painful Problems with Grace and Truth.* Minneapolis: Bethany House, 2019.

Gates, Bill. *How to Avoid a Climate Disaster.* New York: Knopf, 2021.

Generations United. *A Place to Call Home: Building Affordable Housing for Grandfamilies.* 2019. Accessed December 27, 2021. https://www.grandfamilies .org/Portals/0/Documents/General%20Kinship%20Publications/19-Grandfamilies -Report-APlacetoCallHome.pdf.

Gottlieb, Daniel. *Letters to Sam: Lessons on Love, Loss, and the Gifts of Life.* New York: Sterling, 2006.

"Grandparenthood." Encyclopedia.com. Accessed September 1, 2021. https:// www.encyclopedia.com/social-sciences-and-law/sociology-and-social-reform/ sociology-general-terms-and-concepts/grandparent.

Gratton, Brian and Carole Haber, "Three Phases in the History of American Grandparents: Authority, Burden, Companion," *Generations* 20, no.1 (1996) tha]: 13.

Harper, Cavin. *Courageous Grandparenting: Building a Legacy Worth Outliving You.* Revised edition. Colorado Springs: Christian Grandparenting Network, 2018.

Harper, Fletcher. *Green Faith: Mobilizing God's People to Save the Earth.* Nashville: Abingdon Press, 2015.

Harper, Lynn Casteel. *On Vanishing: Mortality, Dementia, and What It Means to Disappear.* New York: Catapult, 2020.

Hayhoe, Katharine. *Saving Us: A Climate Scientist's Case for Hope and Healing in a Divided World.* New York: One Signal, 2021.

Hodgson, Harriet. "Grief's Linking Objects: The Winnowing Process." Open to Hope, November 12, 2016. Accessed November 22, 2021. https://www.opentohope .com/griefs-linking-objects-winnowing-process/.

———. *So, You're Raising Your Grandkids! Tested Tips, Research, and Real-Life Stories to Make Your Life Easier.* WriteLife, 2018.

Horowitz, Juliana Menasce, Nikki Graf, and Gretchen Livingston, "The Landscape of Marriage and Cohabitation in the U.S." Pew Research Center, November 6, 2019. Accessed November 9, 2021. https://www.pewresearch.org/social-trends/2019/11 /06/the-landscape-of-marriage-and-cohabitation-in-the-u-s/.

"How to Adopt a Child." WikiHow. Accessed February 14, 2022. https://www .wikihow.com/Adopt-a-Child.

Isay, Jane. *Unconditional Love: A Guide to Navigating the Joys and Challenges of Being a Grandparent Today.* New York: HarperCollins, 2018.

Jahren, Hope. *The Story of More: How We Got to Climate Change and Where to Go from Here.* New York: Vintage Books, 2020.

James, Christopher. "Every Investor Must Vote." *Time*, January 17/January 24, 2022.

Jenkins, Philip. "Is American Christianity Really in Free Fall?" *Patheos*, October 22, 2019. https://www.patheos.com/blogs/anxiousbench/2019/10/is-american -christianity-really-in-free-fall/.

Kayson, Ronda. "Multi-Generational Helps 'Grandfamilies' Come Together." AARP, March 6, 2020. Accessed December 27, 2021. https://www.aarp.org/home-family/your-home/info-2020/grandfamily-housing.html.

Kimmel, Tim, and Darcy Kimmel. *Extreme Grandparenting: The Ride of Your Life!* Carol Stream, IL: Tyndale House, 2007.

Kolbert, Elizabeth. *The Sixth Extinction: An Unnatural History.* New York: Holt, 2014.

———. *Under a White Sky: The Nature of the Future.* New York: Crown, 2021.

Kornhaber, Arthur. *The Grandparent Guide: The Definitive Guide to Coping with the Challenges of Modern Grandparenting.* Chicago: Contemporary Books, 2002.

———. *The Grandparent Solution: How Parents Can Build a Family Team for Practical, Emotional, and Financial Success.* San Francisco: Jossey-Bass, 2004.

Kornhaber, Arthur, with Sondra Forsyth. *Grandparent Power! How to Strengthen the Vital Connection among Grandparents, Parents, and Children.* New York: Crown, 1994,

Kornhaber, Arthur, and Kenneth L. Woodward. *Grandparents/Grandchildren: The Vital Connection.* New York: Routledge, 2019.

Kunzig, Robert. "The End of Trash." *National Geographic* (March 2020): 42–71.

Lake, Rebecca. "Average Cost of Adoption in the US." *The Balance.* Accessed February 14, 2022. https://www.thebalance.com/average-cost-of-adoption-in-the-u-s-4582452.

Marshall, Joseph. *Walking with Grandfather: The Wisdom of Lakota Elders.* Boulder, CO: Sounds True, 2005.

McClaren, Brian, D. *Faith after Doubt: Why Your Beliefs Stopped Working and What to Do about It.* New York: St. Martin's Essentials, 2021.

McEntyre, Marilyn, and Shirley Showalter. *The Mindful Grandparent: The Art of Loving Our Children's Children.* Minneapolis: Broadleaf Books, 2022.

McKibben, Bill. "The Basic Math of Climate Change." *Sojourners*, March 2021.

Mercadante, Linda. *Belief without Borders: Inside the Minds of the Spiritual but Not Religious.* New York: Oxford University Press, 2014.

Mohr, Jon. "Find Us Faithful." Birdwing Music and Jonathan Mark Music, admin. by Capitol CMG Publishing, 1987.

Morgan Stanley. "When Little Geniuses Have Big Dreams." February 12, 2016. Accessed October 26, 2021. https://www.morganstanley.com/articles/little-geniuses-big-dreams.

"Mother's Day." *Wikipedia.* Accessed January 21, 2022. https://en.wikipedia.org/wiki/Mother%27s_Day.

Mulvihill, Josh. *Biblical Grandparenting: Exploring God's Design for Disciple-Making and Passing Faith to Future Generations.* Minneapolis: Bethany House, 2018.

National Council on Aging. "Money for Older Adults." Accessed November 17, 2019. https://www.ncoa.org/economic-security/money-management/.

Neugarten, Bernice L. and Karol K. Weinstein. "The Changing American Grandparent," *Journal of Marriage and Family* 26, no. 2 (1964): 199–204.

"Old Age Intestate." *Harper's* 162 (May 1931): 712–13.

Olson, Richard P. *Laughter in a Time of Turmoil: Humor as a Spiritual Practice* Eugene, OR: Wipf and Stock, 2012.

Pierce, Yolanda. *In My Grandmother's House: Black Women, Faith, and the Stories We Inherit*. Minneapolis: Broadleaf Press, 2021.

Pilch, John. *The Cultural Dictionary of the Bible*. Collegeville, MN: Liturgical Press, 1999.

Pipher, Mary. *Another Country: Navigating the Emotional Terrain of Our Elders*. New York: Riverhead Books, 1999.

———. *Women Rowing North: Navigating Life's Currents and Flourishing as We Age*. New York: Bloomsbury, 2018.

Powell, Kara and Brad M. Griffin. *3 Big Questions That Change Every Teenager: Making the Most of Your Conversations and Connections*. Grand Rapids: Baker Books, 2021.

Putnam, Robert D. and David E. Campbell, *American Grace: How Religion Divides and Unites Us*. New York: Simon and Schuster, 2010.

Putnam, Robert D., and Shaylyn Romney Garrett. *The Upswing: How America Came Together a Century Ago and How We Can Do It Again*. New York: Simon and Schuster, 2020.

Remen, Rachel Naomi. *My Grandfather's Blessings: Stories of Strength, Refuge, and Belonging*. Thorndike, ME: G.K. Hall, 2001.

Roark, Walter. *Keeping Your Grandkids Alive till Their Ungrateful Parents Arrive: The Guide for Fun-Loving Granddads*. Roswell, GA: Clearing Skies Press, 2004.

Sapp, Stephen. *Full of Years: Aging and the Elderly in the Bible and Today*. Nashville: Abingdon Press, 1987.

Schenkman, Lauren. "Meet a Scientist with a Most Enjoyable Job: He Studies Baby Laughter." TED, June 5, 2019. https://ideas.ted.com/meet-a-scientist-with-a-most-delightful-job-he-studies-baby-laughter/.

Shannon Cloyd, Betty. *Parents and Grandparents as Spiritual Guides: Nurturing Children of the Promise*. Nashville: Upper Room Books, 2000.

Shapiro, Evan. "How Zimbabwean Grandmothers Are Stepping in to Fight Depression." *Time*, February 7, 2019. https://time.com/5523806/friendship-bench-zimbabwe-mental-illness/.

Simons, Rae. *Grandparents Raising Kids*. Broomall, PA: Mason Crest, 2010.

Smith, Christian and Amy Adamczyk. *Handing Down the Faith: How Parents Pass Their Religion on to the Next Generation*. New York: Oxford University Press, 2021.

Smith, Wes. *Hope Meadows: Real-Life Stories of Healing and Caring from an Inspiring Community*. New York: Berkley Books, 2001.

Sollereder, Bethany. "Climate Change Is Here." *Christian Century* 138, no. 19 (September 22, 2021): 24–27.

Springtide Research Institute, *Belonging: Reconnecting America's Loneliest Generation*. Farmington, MN: Springtide Research Institute, 2020.

———. *The State of Religion and Young People: Navigating Uncertainty*. Farmington, MN: Springtide Research Institute, 2021.

Stahl, Lesley. *Becoming Grandma: The Joys and Science of the New Grandparenting*. New York: Blue Rider Press, 2016.

Stassen Berger, Kathleen. *Grandmothering: Building Strong Ties with Every Generation.* Lanham, MD: Rowman & Littlefield, 2019.

Sutton, Jeremy. "Erik Erikson's Stages of Psychosocial Development Explained." *Positive Psychology*, August 5, 2020. Accessed October 21, 2021. https://positivepsychology.com/erikson-stages/.

The Holy Bible Containing the Old and New Testaments: New Revised Standard Version. Nashville: Thomas Nelson, 1989.

The New Testament and Psalms: An Inclusive Version. New York: Oxford University Press, 1995.

The Trevor Project, https://www.thetrevorproject.org/resources?s=Suicide.

Tropp, Laura. *Grandparents in a Digital Age: The Third Act.* Lanham, MD: Lexington Books, 2019.

Viorst, Judith. *I'm Too Young to be Seventy and Other Delusions.* New York: Simon and Schuster, 2005.

———, *Nearing 90 [and Other Comedies of Late Life].* New York: Simon and Schuster, 2019.

———. *Suddenly Sixty: And Other Shocks of Later Life.* New York: Simon and Schuster, 2000.

———. *Unexpectedly Eighty and Other Adaptations.* New York: Free Press, 2010.

Westheimer, Ruth K., and Steven Kaplan. *Grandparenthood.* New York: Routledge, 1998.

Whitt, Ken. *God Is Just Love: Building Spiritual Resilience and Sustainable Communities for the Sake of Our Children and Creation.* Canton, MI: Read the Spirit Books, 2021.

Wiering, Maria, "Pope Francis Declares a Day to Celebrate Grandparents." NextAvenue, July 22, 2021. Accessed July 22, 2021. https://www.nextavenue.org/pope-francis-grandparents-day/.

Wimberly, Anne E. Streaty. "From Intercessory Hope to Mutual Intercession: Grandparents Raising Grandchildren and the Church's Response." *Family Ministry* 14, no. 3 (fall 2000): 19–37.

Witkin, Georgia. *The Modern Grandparent's Handbook: The Ultimate Guide to the New Rules of Grandparenting.* Thorndike, Maine: Center Point Large Print, 2012.

Wyse, Lois. *Grandchildren Are So Much Fun, I Should Have Had Them First.* New York: Crown Trade Paperbacks, 1992.

———. *You Wouldn't Believe What My Grandchild Did . . .* Thorndike, ME: Thorndike Press, 1994.

Young, Susan Lebel. *Grandkids as Gurus: Lessons for Adults.* Just Write Books, 2020.

YWCA. "Child Sexual Abuse Facts." September 2017. Accessed October 25, 2021. https://www.ywca.org/wp-content/uploads/WWV-CSA-Fact-Sheet-Final.pdf.

Zullo, Kathryn, and Allan Zullo. *A Boomer's Guide to Grandparenting.* Kansas City, MO: Andrews McMeel, 2004.

Index of Bible Passages

Index

About the Author

Richard P. Olson has served as pastor or staff member of churches in Massachusetts, South Dakota, Wisconsin, Colorado, and Kansas. He has been a pastoral counselor and a teacher in college. Most recently, in early retirement years, he was the distinguished professor of pastoral theology at Central Baptist Theological Seminary, from which he retired in 2016.

He received his bachelor's degree from Sioux Falls College, MDiv and STM from Andover Newton Theological School, and PhD from Boston University (social ethics). He was also a fellow in the American Association of Pastoral Counselors.

He and Mary Ann, his wife of sixty-five years, have three daughters, six grandchildren, and four great-grandchildren. They have relished their roles with this family. It is out of this journey and conversations with other enthused grandparents and grandchildren that this book was created.

In 2018, they moved to a retirement community, Oakwood Village at Prairie Ridge in Madison, Wisconsin. This move brought them closer to family members and more frequent contact with the grandchildren and great-grandchildren.

This is the twenty-first book for which he is author or coauthor, the most recent being *Laughter in a Time of Turmoil*; *Side by Side: Being Christian in a Multi-faith World*; *A Guide to Ministry Self-Care: Negotiating Today's Challenges with Resilience and Grace*; and *Celebrating the Graying Church: Mutual Ministry Today, Legacies Tomorrow* (the last two are also Rowman & Littlefield publications).